How to

MAKE MONEY GROWING PLANTS, TREES, AND FLOWERS

A Guide to Profitable Earth Friendly Ventures

Francis X. Jozwik

ANDMAR PRESS

Mills, Wyoming 82644

Library of Congress Catalog Card Number 91-75621
ISBN 0-916781-06-2
Printed in the United States of America

Publisher's Cataloging in Publication
(Prepared by Quality Books Inc.)

Jozwik, Francis X.
    How to make money growing plants, trees, and flowers: a guide to
profitable earth friendly ventures / Francis Xavier Jozwik.
    p. cm.
    Includes bibliographical references and index.
    ISBN 0-916781-06-2

    1. Horticulture.   2. Small business—management.   I. Title.

SB50   635
                                              QBI91-1388

CONTENTS

PART I
FUNDAMENTAL RELATIONSHIPS
OF HORTICULTURE
AND BUSINESS

Chapter 1   Introduction to the Horticultural Industry..........3
Chapter 2   The Business of Business Is Business............23
Chapter 3   The First Steps of a New Business...........31

PART II
MONEY MAKING
BUSINESSES
IN HORTICULTURE

Chapter 4   Production and Marketing of
             Greenhouse Ornamentals......................41
Chapter 5   Production and Marketing of Ornamental
             Nursery Plants Grown Outdoors.............71
Chapter 6   Production and Marketing of Ornamental
             Perennial Plants.........................95
Chapter 7   The Retail Horticultural Business..............105
Chapter 8   Additional Horticultural Speciality Businesses.............109

PART III
HOW TO GET STARTED
AND SUCCEED IN BUSINESS

Chapter 9   Collect Information and Develop a Plan.........127
Chapter 10   Selling at a Profit 135
Chapter 11   The Ingredients for Business Success 161
Chapter 12   How to Finance a New Business 165
Chapter 13   Coping With Success.............173

Suggested Literature 175
Index........179
Book Ordering Information.........184

About the Author

Francis Jozwik received a Ph.D. in Plant Science from the University of Wyoming in 1966. He began his professional career lecturing in plant physiology with the University of Wisconsin System and later was appointed to the position of Arid Lands Research Scientist in the Commonwealth Scientific and Industrial Research Organization of Australia.

In addition to his scientific and academic background, Dr. Jozwik has become active in commercial horticulture as the owner of a successful greenhouse and nursery business. The wide experience Dr. Jozwik has acquired both as a scientist and in private industry assure that his books and articles are technically correct while possessing a down-to-earth style.

Readers of the present book who wish to investigate specific details of commercial ornamental plant culture more thoroughly will find a larger volume by Dr. Jozwik useful for further study; it is entitled *The Greenhouse and Nursery Handbook*. Ordering information is available near the back cover.

Disclaimer

This book is intended to present information about commercial activity within certain subject areas of horticulture. While the author and publisher have carefully attempted to make this information reliable and timely, readers should note that a good deal of it is based upon personal experiences and observations of the author. The validity of the information and viewpoints can differ with circumstances; therefore, neither the author or publisher guarantees the accuracy of the text material under all situations.

No attempt has been made to make the present book a final and ultimate source of information about the subject matter involved. Readers should always study further sources in order to complement, amplify, and confirm the present text.

Beginning a business in specialized horticulture is not a get rich quick scheme. Although many people have become extremely successful in this field, most have accomplished the feat only after working hard and smart.

The author and Andmar Press shall have no liability or responsibility to any individual or entity experiencing loss or damage or alleged loss or damage thought to be caused directly or indirectly by information presented in this book.

Readers who do not wish to accept the above conditions in full may feel free to return this book to the publisher for a refund of the purchase price.

Part I

FUNDAMENTAL RELATIONSHIPS OF HORTICULTURE AND BUSINESS

Hello, my name is Francis Jozwik. The book you are now reading, called *Make Money Growing Plants, Trees, and Flowers*, results from more than twenty years of my experience as a commercial grower of ornamental plants. I hope you will find it indispensable as a practical guide which helps you get started successfully in some aspect of the horticultural business.

Make Money Growing Plants, Trees, and Flowers is oriented towards people who wish to begin in this business with as little monetary risk as possible. Therefore, most of the information presented will deal with situations applicable to small start up ventures rather than to larger, more complex enterprises. This book is meant to be used by ordinary people who want to grow plants for profit. Highly technical production and marketing methods are not emphasized since they generally have little relevance to the initial stages of a new business.

The information you need now to get started is quite different from what you may need later to address the more concrete problems of day to day business operation. Several specialized horticultural publications which will help you in this regard are listed in the Suggested Literature section at the back of this book.

In *Make Money Growing Plants, Trees, and Flowers* I do not focus upon specifics about how to grow plants for a profit. My objective at the moment is to provide the beginner with a concise and easily read overview which highlights important points quickly. In this way readers will hopefully maintain a creative frame of mind unhindered by over attention to detail. I want to help you choose an area of horticultural business in which to specialize and then show you how to start a profitable operation as easily as possible.

I trust you will find the information presented in the following pages to be both interesting and profitable. Horticulture is a tremendously satisfying field which abounds with opportunity. Keep in mind that many million dollar horticultural businesses were born in the backyard of enterprising individuals just like you.

Chapter 1

INTRODUCTION TO THE HORTICULTURAL INDUSTRY

Horticulture is not a particularly exact word. One person might place a topic within the confines of agriculture or perhaps botany, while another would argue that it properly belongs in horticulture. Most dictionaries describe horticulture as dealing with the activity of growing fruits, vegetables, flowers, or ornamentals. It is frequently referred to as both a science and an art. This definition agrees fairly well with the meaning of horticulture in this book, but with the important qualification that the areas of flowers and ornamentals will be emphasized more than those of fruits and vegetables.

This reduction in the scope of the topic is due partially to the limited expertise which I possess, but it mainly results from the fact that flowers and ornamentals are the highest value crops which are widely cultured. Consequently they offer the business person a better chance of good monetary returns even if only a limited number of plants are grown.

Certain topics dealing with vegetable and fruit production are included in this book but they will be limited to those cases where production takes place under cover (greenhouse) or at least in very intensively managed outdoor facilities.

The types of horticulture I want to concentrate on as potential business projects are those which require a good deal of specialized knowledge and control of crop conditions.

Success in specialized horticultural crops depends to a large part upon knowledge rather than upon generous amounts of luck, land, and money; which are the hallmarks of traditional field crops.

A person armed with little more than a few hundred dollars and the right knowledge can still start a profitable greenhouse or nursery. Contrast this with the hundreds of acres of high priced land and expensive field machinery needed to run a modest farm. An investment of one million dollars and more is commonly required for a traditional farm operation which supports a modern family in reasonable comfort.

HORTICULTURE AN EXPANDING INDUSTRY

Ornamental horticulture in the United States is a booming industry and, as with any dynamic situation, there are lots of opportunities for enterprising individuals. The demand for ornamental plants is generated mainly by trends in national lifestyle which will continue unabated. Everyone is becoming more ecologically minded and more fully aware of the ethical and practical benefits which ornamental plants can add to human life and the environment. Reinforcing this change in basic national psychology is the fact that, generally, both husband and wife now work outside the home; this increases household income but reduces the time available for outdoor and indoor gardening activities.

People want to enjoy plants and flowers more but they have less time to do it. Professional horticulturists can now command an excellent income by providing the time saving goods and services which consumers demand. Ornamental horticulture is no longer an infant industry which supplies only the basics of seed, fertilizer, and perhaps a few bare root shrubs and trees; a large volume and varied assortment of sophisticated horticultural supplies and services have become more or less necessities of life to many people.

Tasteful landscaping consistently ranks as the least costly method of improving home values. This fact helps commercial horticulturists sell billions of dollars worth of goods and services each year.

ROOM FOR INDIVIDUALS IN HORTICULTURE

Fortunately for the individual entrepreneur, relatively little of the horticultural production industry has been invaded by large corporations. Only in the area of hardgoods, such as fertilizer and pots, have they made significant inroads. Anywhere there is money to be made we can expect corporate management to investigate the possibilities; but the inherent variability of plants, their need for constant care, and the diversity of environments in which they are utilized is not the ideal situation for the standardized methods which megabusiness is best at.

Large national corporations have tried to enter the plant growing segment of horticulture but have, in general, pulled back out as they find that producing living organisms is more complicated than manufacturing stoves and refrigerators. By far the greatest total number of greenhouses and nurseries

The garden products section of a major discount chain. Similar set ups in supermarkets, department stores, and other mass market outlets account for perhaps one half of horticultural sales. This particular display is neat and offers a reasonable selection of merchandise. Often rare qualities in this type of merchandising.

throughout the United States are small to medium size and are owned by individuals who sell a good deal of their product through their own retail outlet. Even the larger production facilities are most frequently owned by individuals or closely held companies.

Marketing of greenhouse and nursery crops was formerly accomplished almost entirely through the producer's own retail facility or through numerous independent florists and garden stores. At present, a large part of ornamental plant products are sold by chain, discount, and food stores. Hardware and department stores also do a significant amount of business.

For live plants and cutflowers as a whole, perhaps a little less than half are now sold through the non traditional outlets; of course this figure will vary greatly depending

A medium sized retail bedding plant greenhouse and tree nursery. Individually owned operations like this account for about one half of retail horticultural sales. Most consumers consistently prefer to purchase garden products at these full service outlets, even though prices are generally higher than at self service locations.

upon the exact nature of the product, geography, and demographic factors. Twenty or thirty years ago independent operations were caught unprepared to market effectively against chain type competition; but at present the independents seem to have adapted well and may even be benefiting from the wide and constant public exposure which flowers and plants receive in mass outlets.

Those independent retailers who have placed their emphasis upon service, high quality, and new or unusual products seem to flourish now while the ones who tried to compete head on in price terms with mass outlets have fallen by the wayside. And many growers of ornamentals have seized the opportunity to supply chain type outlets. Of course these growers must adapt to the mass market philosophy of high volume and generally lower price for the product. Often times in this situation, quality has suffered. Chains pressure the grower for lower and lower prices until factors essential for proper plant growth are sacrificed. Fortunately most people in the industry have begun to realize the folly of this situation and, in general, chain buyers are stressing quality more than in the past.

We may summarize the general situation in ornamental horticulture by saying that it is an industry whose exceptional growth is due to fundamental and continuing changes in national psychology and living patterns. Individuals and small companies dominate the plant growing segment while activity in the marketing phase is split fairly evenly between chain outlets and independent operators. Although plants and flowers are often distributed nationally, market prices are still determined primarily by local factors and participants are more or less able to fix their own prices by providing differing levels of quality, service, and selection. Ornamental plants, trees, and flowers offer an exceptional opportunity for good profits while the monetary requirements for starting in business are generally much lower than in the traditional commodity oriented segments of agriculture and horticulture.

BASIC ORGANIZATIONAL PATTERNS IN HORTICULTURAL SPECIALITIES

If you carefully recollected the specific activity or combination of activities of each horticultural business you have visited over the years and classified these memories into logical order, I believe you would arrive at basically the same industry organizational patterns which I will soon outline. In the process you would, of course, find that there are many hybrid operations which do not fall neatly into any one area of activity. Although I will explore each particular horticultural specialty area in more detail later, readers will benefit from having a concise preview of the industry right from the start.

Production

The production phase of horticultural specialty crops is a rather obvious aspect of the industry; but perhaps only a few readers have observed firsthand the actual workings of such a growing facility. Your closest experience with production operations most likely would be with a small neighborhood greenhouse or nursery, which was growing a portion of its merchandise needs while buying the rest from wholesale specialists. You are not likely to have visited the production locations of larger independent retailers or wholesale growers. Generally, the managers of these larger production operations must, out of necessity, limit the number of visitors so that work may continue without interruption.

Production facilities for horticultural specialty crops are as diverse as the particular needs of each crop and the ingenuity of individuals growing it. There are different ways to solve cultural requirements and the chosen solution may vary with the materials available, climate, financing, individual inclination, and marketing objectives. The atmosphere at a production facility may range from one of complete dependence upon technical methods to the opposite attitude where success or failure depends upon vague "feelings" the grower may have about the needs of crops. Fortunately, most modern growers lean towards the first alternative as they become aware of the competitive advantages offered by efficient, reliable crop production methods.

The size of production facilities in specialized horticultural crops ranges from tiny backyard setups to gigantic operations. Most fall into the small or medium size range. There has been some tendency of late (particularly in the greenhouse field) for firms to expand quickly. This is only natural when growers see attractive markets without an adequate supply of products. But many growers have found that bigness does not necessarily lead to greater profits and stability. Now some growers are beginning to question the wisdom of extremely rapid growth and are concentrating more upon profitability rather than volume.

The primary driving forces for change in the production aspects of horticultural specialty crops are the decrease in availability of cheap labor and the virtual explosion in technological knowledge which is taking place. Any present day grower who does not take advantage of labor saving techniques and who does not keep abreast of new knowledge in the field will soon find that it is impossible to compete with more progressive operations. It is absolutely essential for growers to keep themselves informed about all aspects of the industry so that they may organize their production towards the most efficient use of resources.

Marketing

The important point to be made about marketing in horticultural specialty crops is that, luckily, it generally lacks a centralized character. Centralized marketing, whether it results from government, industry, or financial interests always tends to limit the ability of individuals to determine and ask for the price they feel is proper for their merchandise. Centralized markets such as auctions and government and industry sponsored marketing authorities represent an easy means for growers to sell crops. But the passive acceptance of whatever price marketing organizations allow does not usually lead to the highest possible profits for better growers. Centralized markets function best when a product possesses relatively uniform characteristics. If growers must tailor their produce to meet these uniform standards, then there is little room left for individuals who wish to distinguish their product in the public eye. This is the primary reason why food and fiber farmers have generally realized low profit levels from their operations. Within the different classes of corn which have been established by market authorities, each farmer in a region receives basically the same price at any given time. There is little incentive for product differentiation under these conditions; in fact, there is a bias against any variation.

A similar situation exists for most major commodity crops. So while centralized marketing may function as a lubricant to effective national trading and distribution, it rarely benefits innovative growers who wish to offer products which differ from the standard version. In my role as a grower of ornamental plants and flowers I have often wished that I could be spared the necessity of always finding a profitable market for my plants. This is the most difficult part of my job and I would much rather spend time immersed in the delightful task of growing beautiful crops. However, when the yearly accounting of profits is done, I give thanks that conscientious and knowledgeable growers like myself are able to ask for and receive prices which are much higher than the ordinary. Growing plants for a living is fun but it soon becomes stale when the monetary rewards are slim or nonexistent. Creating profitable market channels through active participation in the selling process takes time, thought, and advance planning; but it is well worth the trouble.

A marketing plan is necessary for anyone who wishes to grow plants for a profit. You must sell what you raise if you hope to stay in business. The financial success of horticultural specialty crop growers is usually determined more by their ability to market crops effectively rather than by their prowess as growers. The proper order of business is first to devise a marketing strategy and plan of implementation and then grow the crop. I must emphasize that proceeding in the opposite manner is the most common mistake of unsuccessful growers. It is possible to build a successful career in horticulture simply by selling what others produce; you need not grow a single plant. In fact, the marketing phase of horticultural specialty crops is normally a more financially rewarding endeavor than is growing the plants. There are several areas of horticultural business, such as flower shops and garden centers, where no crops are generally grown; the operation serves strictly or predominantly as a marketing entity. For people who possess the talent to market effectively, this type of operation often offers a means of entering the

The basic bedding plant display at supermarkets reduces garden products to the status of common commodities. Quality and price are generally on the low end.

industry with less monetary resources than is necessary to begin actual crop production.

I have previously mentioned the essential points about where and by whom most horticultural specialty crops are sold. It is obvious that marketing of these crops is evolving a two tier structure. At the bottom are the mass outlets who deal primarily in products which are treated more or less as commodities; that is, those which are sold in volume, those which exhibit some degree of uniformity within classes and can be easily handled and priced, and those which require a minimum of service. On the second tier are the independent outlets which deal in more than strictly the commonplace plants and products and which offer a maximum of service. This two tier merchandising system is evolving because of natural forces in the market place. I suggest that you recognize the reality of it and search for a place to fit in rather than trying to "buck" the system. You as an independent will not be financially successful if you try to compete in volume and price with a nationwide chain; and mass outlets will likely fail if they try to offer a myriad of special products and services.

Similar plant varieties as in the preceding photograph but tastefully combined into planter arrangements which excite the customer's imagination. Independent horticulturists can command top prices for beautiful material like this.

Services

Many of you will wonder why I am now preparing to discuss services as part of a book about growing plants and flowers for a profit. I think if you stop and mentally imagine various businesses which have some connection to horticulture you will find that some of them offer very little in the way of tangible plant products; they sell a service, such as landscape design, plant care, or pest control. These are the more obvious aspects of service in the industry, but there is some degree of service offered with almost every plant sale. Even the least service oriented mass outlets provide care tags with plants to help customers enjoy their purchase. And at the other end of the spectrum, the price of plants or flowers at some upscale specialty shops is mainly dictated by the amount of special service connected with the purchase. Some outlets for horticultural products do not have a clear vision of the relationship which connects products and services. They do not know what they are selling. This type of confused situation can lead to disastrous consequences through not pricing merchandise to include the cost of services rendered, aiming products at the wrong economic class of purchasers, and many more merchandising mistakes. Smart marketers learn to evaluate service factors correctly and how to best use them to advantage in particular business situations.

In the future, the marketing aspect of horticultural products by independent operators will increasingly be dominated by those who are devising creative ways to provide needed services along with the plant products they wish to sell. The days when a grower could simply offer marigold and petunia seedlings or bare root nursery stock and expect consumers to knock down the door are over. Customers desire and need added services to satisfy new lifestyles. They will go someplace else if you don't provide what they want.

Integration of production, marketing, and service

At this point you may be slightly confused by my description of the three different areas of activity within the industry. You are perhaps asking yourself why a book entitled *Make Money Growing Plants, Trees, and Flowers* should be emphasizing that the future lies in developing market skills and providing services; or that the real opportunities for individuals to make money lie not so much in growing horticultural specialty crops but in these related follow up activities. This emphasis in no way downgrades the importance of the plant growing activities in the industry but merely recognizes the fact that modern producers must also be reasonably proficient in the marketing and service sectors in order to become successful. Quality plants will always be the keystone of the industry but they certainly do not comprise the entire picture.

An individual or firm can prosper and expand while exclusively engaged in production, or marketing, or horticultural services. But most operations successfully combine two or more aspects in greater or lesser degree. The most stable, prosperous, and enjoyable operations to manage are those which are fairly completely integrated in a vertical manner. That is to say, the operation produces the plants, provides the necessary services, and markets the combination to the end consumer. This is the ideal situation in which a business controls all the factors which are within it's sphere of influence. Of course there are always factors such as climate, the national economy, and chance occurrences which no business can hope to influence. This book will be premised upon the assumption that whatever particular horticultural business venture you might engage in, it will be vertically integrated to the maximum degree possible under the prevailing circumstances.

WHY AND WHERE TO START IN HORTICULTURE

There are two primary reasons why a person should contemplate going into a particular field of business. First, the individual must, by underlying nature, hold a strong and abiding interest in the subject matter; second, the field must offer a reasonable chance of monetary success. No one I know wants to spend their time doing something which holds no interest for them and no one I know wants to run a business which doesn't make money.

Given the obvious nature of these two reasons for entering a business field, it is amazing how many people become involved in a venture which lacks one or the other, or both essential characteristics. I hope that after reading this book, you will be able to intelligently decide whether a horticultural specialty area can fulfill both necessary attributes when your particular situation is addressed.

I have mentioned, in a general way, some horticultural areas which lend themselves to business activity. Perhaps now is the best time to point out specific enterprises which you may wish to consider and which will be discussed more fully in later chapters. Some of these possible ventures are more widely applicable while others might be suitably adapted to only a few special situations. You are the only person who can decide which most closely fits your interests, capabilities, and business environment. The list of likely enterprises in Table 1 is by no means exhaustive and should be interpreted only as a starting point for inquiry. You will notice quickly that many of these business areas could be combined into a single operation if the proper circumstances were available.

There is no magic formula for deciding which horticultural specialty to engage in. Basically you want to choose one which emphasizes the strong points of your personal situation while minimizing any weak points. Study the business activities in Table 1 so that as you read further, you will be able to relate particular information presented to individual

Table 1

Some specific business activities in specialized horticulture. One or more activities may often be included in the same operation.

A. Greenhouse ornamentals for indoor and outdoor decoration.
B. Nursery ornamentals, mainly outdoor production.
C. Retail sales only, can include any aspect of specialized horticulture.
D. Perennial plant specialist, mainly herbaceous landscape plants.
E. Greenhouse vegetable, fresh fruit, and greens production for ordinary consumption.
F. Greenhouse herbs and unusual vegetables, either fresh or dried for use in specialized serving and cooking situations.
G. Market gardens, direct to consumer outdoor production of fruit and vegetables. Sometimes includes herb and flower production.
H. Herbs and medicinal plant production, outdoor culture for wholesale distributors.
I. Seed production for specialty crops.
J. Mail order specialist, mostly concentrated in sales of dormant herbaceous and woody landscape plants but can be any crop.
K. Outdoor and interior landscape, may include only design and consultation services but usually entails plant sales and installation.
L. Interior plant care, usually business and public installations.
M. Exterior plant care, ranges from simple lawn jobs to extensive technical services.
N. Lawn sod and plug production, may also include installation.
O. Wildflower seed and plant production, concentration upon those species perceived to represent less domesticated entities for a climatic area.
P. Christmas tree production and sales, may include associated Christmas items.
Q. Horticultural therapy and learning services. Clients may be at a disadvantage physically or mentally or may require only a normal learning or recreational program.

areas which you find interesting. Don't try to make any final selection at this point. As you become more familiar with different subject matter, it is likely your mind will unconsciously be guided toward the best possible choice for you. And at some point you will spontaneously realize what it is you want to concentrate your efforts upon. Let things happen naturally, don't force a decision. Most people who have read this book to the present point must have a serious interest in horticultural topics. And accordingly, these readers, either from practical experience or from reading or education, probably possess considerable knowledge about the subject. This is a definite advantage if you want to get into business for yourself. Why not start in a field in which you have inherent interests and talents? Many of the basic requirements for success in commercial horticulture will seem like second nature to you if you have already amassed an extensive knowledge about the subject.

I have always been interested in plants and many years ago I became a university professor and researcher in plant science. This occupation proved to be reasonably satisfying but it always seemed as if my life was somewhat sterile and lacked a strong feeling of contact with nature and my own subconscious needs. After a few years working as a scientist, I simply arrived at a rather immediate decision to quit and start my own greenhouse business. As time has passed, I now understand some of the forces which led me to that fortunate decision.

Many persons, like myself, are interested in plants primarily for the beauty and harmony expressed in the existence of these organisms rather than the intellectual stimulation which results from a careful study of their chemical and physical properties. Horticulture has allowed me to live a life filled with both intellectual satisfaction and with an artistic joy which proceeds from my work with beautiful living creations.

Also, I find that the competitive stimulation of commercial life and the healthy physical work often required in horticulture serve as an elixir which purely intellectual activities cannot match.

The personal feelings I have just described may or may not be reasons which have some influence upon your decision to start a horticultural business. For those individuals who feel some kinship to such things, perhaps you

The family business is a good place to start learning and earning. The author's daughter, pictured above, enjoys her work in the greenhouse while making money for future college expenses. Monika also did the word processing for the book you are now reading.

will find it reassuring that feelings such as these can be a positive practical advantage for anyone entering horticultural business. It certainly doesn't hurt to have a spiritual life which is in tune with the practical activities of earning a living.

Now let us examine a few hardheaded business reasons which show why growing plants or flowers or other specialty crops might be a profitable venture for you. Gardening of various types is the most popular leisure activity in America. Couple this with the demand for horticultural produce which accumulates from floral use, the food industry, and other miscellaneous sources and you can easily see that horticulture is a large and broadly based field; some commercial horticultural activity can be found in almost every neighborhood in the country. There is opportunity everywhere, not just in particular population centers.

Since the utilization of special horticultural crops is predominantly tied to leisure time, special events, or luxury consumption; purchasers seldom have price uppermost in mind as they shop. They are looking for that special plant, Christmas tree, or the most succulent tomato which will help to make their life more enjoyable. This situation provides high profits for those horticulturists who are able to efficiently and tastefully supply the special needs of their targeted market population. As I have mentioned previously, the price of special horticultural products to end consumers may be many times that which is justifiable upon material costs alone. Specialized horticulture is characterized by high markups on merchandise. A smart operator in this field can make lots of money without a huge initial or continuing investment.

Of course you can seldom expect to start a successful business without investing some money. I don't want to give you the wrong impression by suggesting that you can profitably start growing and selling specialty crops with only the shirt on your back. Any venture you decide upon will require at least a minimum investment to get started and, depending upon how fancy you want to get, some will cost a lot. What I wish to emphasize is that, due to various factors, it is much cheaper to get started commercially in specialized horticulture than almost any other field. That is if you don't mind working hard and are willing to acquire the necessary specialized knowledge! I can't motivate you to work hard but I can supply you with much of the information you need to succeed.

Some aspects of horticulture are so ridiculously inexpensive in which to get a commercial toehold that there is no excuse for even lower income persons to say they can't afford to get started. Under the right circumstances you can literally turn a few cents worth of seeds into hundreds of dollars worth of plants that people are anxious to buy. All it takes is time and effort. Later in this book I will go into more detail about some of these possible ventures.

The rags to riches possibilities just mentioned are based upon practical experience in my own business and the hundreds of success stories I have observed personally over the years. Any person who is highly motivated and has a sincere interest can succeed in a commercial horticulture business.

Another factor which might bear upon your entry and continued success in specialized horticulture is that, except in certain circumstances, there isn't a whole lot of foreign competition to deal with. Horticultural produce is often heavy and cannot normally be shipped profitably from country to country. Besides, disease and insect quarantine laws are tightly enforced and greatly restrict the free flow of imports. Sometimes, because of transport problems, you may face little competition even from operations only a few miles away.

I could write many more pages about general advantages characteristic of specialized horticulture, but I think you will benefit more by moving along so that we may soon investigate several concrete examples of interesting specific enterprises. Hopefully I can help develop your knowledge to the point where you can make an informed decision about venturing into this thriving and exciting industry.

Chapter 2

THE BUSINESS OF BUSINESS IS BUSINESS

Certain basic factors should be considered by anyone who is thinking about starting a business, no matter what the nature of the product or services which may be involved. Only those who have started and operated their own independent business can truly appreciate the massive effect this experience has upon the life of the person involved. Therefore, each individual must take such an important step carefully and with eyes wide open.

WHAT IS A BUSINESS?

The first point we must be perfectly clear about is: exactly what definition is to be given the word business? In the sense which we are using in this book, I take business to mean "a series of actions or processes in which people engage to realize a monetary profit." There are various qualifying remarks which we may wish to place upon this definition, such as: at what times during the lifespan of a business must it be profitable to qualify as a true business venture? The Internal Revenue Service is acutely interested in this point. I believe the IRS expects a business to be profitable one out of every four years to be eligible for tax treatment in this category unless extenuating circumstances can be proven to apply. Particularly in the start up phases of a business or in prolonged general economic downturns, it is not uncommon to find companies which operate at a deficit for several years running. But by whatever details of definition which we restrict or expand upon the word, I think most of you will accept, in broad terms, the meaning which I have placed before you.

So we may see that whatever similarities a business possesses with other activities in our life, it is always characterized by the attempt to make a monetary profit. Many people who say they are in business are really engaging in a hobby or recreation. Their chief objective in these cases is to occupy their time with interesting or stimulating activities, not to earn a profit. In some cases we find that individuals successfully combine business, hobby, and recreation. Certainly this is the most desirable circumstance. Some will argue that amassing money is not the sole object of business. And I agree! But we must have a primary objective by which to measure our definition or the attempt becomes meaningless.

I am spending so much effort to clear up our understanding of the word business because I think it is crucial for anyone who becomes involved in such an activity to understand exactly what it is they wish to accomplish. If you want to alter the definition which I have offered, by all means do so; but be aware of the change in goals and objectives which this alteration necessarily imposes upon you. I have observed many unhappy people who, although thinking they are in business, are actually engaging in recreational and hobby activities which almost certainly preclude any chance of profit. Yet they still continue to measure their success or failure by a profit yardstick. If they would look at their activities differently; that is to say, with no connection to profits, they might find that their activities (and their life) were indeed enjoyable and satisfactory. If business, hobbies, and recreation are to be combined satisfactorily into a single activity, each component must be given its due importance and consideration in the overall objectives of the undertaking.

So before you think seriously about getting into business, do some soul searching. Decide exactly what it is that will make your life more enjoyable and how you think this may best be accomplished. Define goals carefully and see if they make sense when considering the circumstances under which you live. In short, give careful consideration to the old adage "know thyself."

Not only must you evaluate how a business venture will affect your own individual life, but the impact upon the lives of others who are closely associated with you must be considered. Here we are speaking primarily of family members or those who have a legal connection of some sort to you. The long hours and material sacrifices often required to get a venture off the ground can be extremely taxing to personal relationships. And the money aspects of business must be viewed with an eye towards the legal implications involved. Most people have some small appreciation of how difficult it is to begin a successful business but not many recognize that getting out of business can be agonizing both monetarily and psychologically, particularly if the venture has proven unsuccessful after a lengthy and costly attempt. This is just one more reason to thoroughly think through any decision about going into business. I am not trying to discourage anyone, in fact I am trying to offer the encouragement and information you need; but it would be less than honest to neglect pointing out some of the more sobering aspects of venturing into a commercial pursuit.

LEARN DETAILS OF PLANNED BUSINESS FIELD

Now let's assume that you have carefully evaluated the general comments just presented and still think you are interested in starting a horticultural business; but being the cautious type, you want to gather more information in order to make the most prudent final decision possible. Where and how can you get the information you need? Some of the more useful sources you might utilize will be pointed out in the following discussion.

My all time favorite suggestion for learning about a field of business is: learn and earn at the same time. Go to work in the chosen industry in any capacity for which there is an opening, even if it means being the least respected and lowest paid member of the organization. You can have your laughs later when you start a successful competing operation. Right now the main objective is to learn as much as possible by the fastest and least expensive method. Working for someone else will normally be the best way to accomplish this. And while you are working, try to gain as wide a background as possible; volunteer for all types of duties, no matter how distasteful. Each new experience will save you money and time in the future. There is simply no better training available for the new business person than actually working in the field. And you get paid for it!

Of course you can't learn everything you need to know by working for someone else. Who knows, they might be doing a lot of things wrong. If you didn't find this out by picking up additional information from other sources you might go on for years in your own business, repeating the errors of a previous employer.

Another valuable fact finding tool is to visit all the existing businesses you can in the same general field. A lot of new ideas will be picked up this way. The best method of making a fact finding mission is to do a lot of looking and listening and then make up your own mind about the implications of your observations. Don't advertise that you plan to be in competition and don't rely much on what someone tells you, they may be mistaken or just making idle talk to pass the time.

Speaking to people in other fields of business is more likely to yield straight answers. They don't view you as a competitor. Remember, you need knowledge not only about your own specialty but on how to do business in general. Local businesses will be able to advise you about the immediate climate for your new venture. Of course you must still use caution to interpret what you hear from these people.

Several private and government agencies probably offer either free or low cost business advice and counseling in your town. The Small Business Administration, farm loan boards, economic development boards, The Chamber of Commerce, banks, and higher educational facilities are but a few of the obvious sources for help. You may find that these people are perhaps not so enthusiastic about your project as you are since they are not personally involved and because, by their very nature, organizations such as these tend to become cautious. They will emphasize formal business plans and ask for quantitative data about production, marketing, and financing. But if your planned venture can't stand careful scrutiny by the bankers and bureaucrats, perhaps it is prudent for you to give it a second look.

There are private business consultants for hire but they are expensive. And the advice they are prepared to give will likely apply to larger and more formally structured operations than the one you will begin. Besides, you can usually buy a book for under fifty dollars that will give similar information in more detail.

I am a firm believer in the value of higher education. But let's face it, the true value of advanced education lies not in preparing an individual for a particular job but in molding a society of individuals who have acquired the ability to think logically and critically in a variety of circumstances. So my advice is that if you wish to lead a more fulfilling life in general or if you have plans to advance further than a small private business, formal education may certainly be helpful, but it is seldom a cost effective method for small private business people to learn the details about a new business venture they plan to start. Notice I said cost effective. You can probably learn what you need to know through formal education; but couldn't you have done it more quickly and economically by other methods? Certain avenues to higher education are quite inexpensive. Night school or community college courses which you can fit into your normal working schedule are examples. But a degree program at an out of town college or university can easily cost $25000.00 per year in lost wages, room and board, and fees.

Every industry has trade shows, conferences, seminars, and professional publications. The world of specialized horticulture certainly is awash in them. And they are invaluable to the newcomer. Publications are the most cost effective way by far to learn about the industry. For less than the cost of your daily newspaper you can subscribe to three or four industry magazines and keep abreast of all the new plant varieties, products, prices, and research developments in your field. Most of the books you need will be available in a nearby public library and the ones that aren't may be purchased at a relatively low cost. The suggested literature section at the back of this book contains some publications which should be considered for your private library.

Trade shows and seminars are expensive, especially if out of town, but tremendously enlightening. If you have time to wait, keep an eye on the industry calender in trade magazines and very likely you will find shows or other gatherings which will take place periodically in the nearest large city to you. Trade shows enable you to evaluate a lot of products and services and make business contacts quickly. The value of educational seminars and conferences varies widely, depending upon the quality and nature of presentations.

EVALUATE INFORMATION GATHERED

After you have made a reasonable effort to educate yourself about business in general and about your particular field of interest, examine all the information realistically. Try to avoid looking at your plan with rose colored glasses. Quantify information whenever possible, numbers are less likely to lead you astray than are vague impressions and general statements. Write down all your important conclusions. You will want to refer to this information later. Now comes the moment of truth! Does all the investigation and preparation still indicate that your business will fly? If not, you had better weigh the risks and benefits more carefully before jumping in with both feet. See if there may be some way to test your venture without an all out commitment of time and resources.

An advertisement for one of the major professional horticultural organizations. You can learn a lot in a hurry by attending meetings such as this. Copy courtesy of Professional Plant Growers Association.

The final decision is yours alone to make. You cannot gather enough information to assure a completely error free choice. So the final leap will always remain an expression of your personal desires and beliefs. Don't force a decision, if you turn the question around in your head enough the answer will usually come without conscious effort. You will simply know what it is you must do.

Let me say one more thing before we pass on to the next topic. Some of the greatest inventions, revolutions in thought, and material achievements of man would not have been accomplished by the people responsible if they had paid much attention to negative information which indicated that their projects were hopeless. If you still feel competent to begin a business in horticulture after your investigation shows it has little likelihood of success, go ahead and do it but make the plunge with a clear understanding of the odds you face.

Chapter 3

THE FIRST STEPS OF A NEW BUSINESS

Now that you have decided to go into business and you think that horticultural specialties may well be the most opportune field; what is the next step towards making this dream a reality? I believe you must focus attention upon a definite niche within this diverse industry. No business could operate successfully in all the various activities of specialized horticulture. You must specialize even further in order to concentrate available time and resources upon a manageable undertaking.

CHOOSING A FIELD OF SPECIALIZATION

Three important questions must be answered by you in the process of choosing a definite business activity area. First, what field of activity interests you the most? This is the key question. No one can for long put forth the tremendous effort necessary to start a business if they are not fervently interested in the field. If you can't decide between two or three possibilities, perhaps this means you should combine them into a single larger enterprise—a quite common solution. Second, which of the choices looks like it will make the most money with the least effort? Let's face it, we are talking about business, not a recreational or charity activity. Monetary success will be one of the primary measures of how good you are as a business person. Third, what is possible with the circumstances under which you live? Although a certain field of activity may interest you the most and appear as though it will make the most money, it may be nearly impossible to consider because it clashes with unchangeable aspects of your present life. You may have to settle for second choice under these circumstances. Life doesn't work out in the best possible way all the time, you must make compromises.

THE QUESTION OF PARTNERS

People are social animals. They live together, eat together, fight together, and love together. Isn't it natural that they should be in business together? Perhaps so but there are some important things you should consider before taking on a business partner. In some respects, a business partner has more call upon your time, financial assets, and future happiness than does a partner in marriage. It is often almost impossible to disassociate oneself from an unsuitable business partner without major financial and legal difficulties.

So why would anyone want a partner? Well, some people just don't like to do anything by themselves. And I suppose this is a good enough reason to take on a business partner if you really feel strongly about it. Personally, I believe the wisest course is to avoid partners unless they definitely add specific mental or material assets which are critical to the success of the venture. The decision to become partners with someone must be evaluated with an eye to the future. People seldom stay the same over long periods of time and your agreeable partner of today may become the Frankenstein of later years. Almost everyone suffers some major personal problems over a lifetime which will significantly affect close associates or family. Can you deal with that? Although business partners can be a joy; like a good spouse, they must be chosen carefully for the long haul.

INVENTORY OF RESOURCES AND LIABILITIES

Good business persons must be constantly aware of the material, monetary, and mental assets of the operation they manage. And they must keep good track of the liabilities, both actual and potential, to which the business is subject. A good part of a manager's job is to make sure that the sum total of assets always equals or exceeds actual and potential liabilities. This is a difficult balancing act because it is not always possible to match like with like in both sides of the equation. You must often assign a common value measure to different assets and liabilities so they may be related logically to one another.

An accurate inventory of assets and liabilities is especially important for someone just starting out in business. You simply must know what you have to work with before you can make any intelligent decisions. The best way of accurately visualizing your situation is to write down all your actual assets in one column and actual liabilities in another. Then assign numerical values from one to ten to each liability or asset. Total the numbers in each column to see if your assets outweigh liabilities. This exercise accomplishes several purposes. It makes you think carefully about just what your assets and liabilities are, it makes you compare their relative values, and it lets you know what the overall situation is. You can do the same thing for assets and liabilities which are not yet in existence but which are likely to be a reality in the near future. Potential assets and liabilities can be used in your assessments of total net values but they certainly shouldn't be given equal weight with present actualities.

Don't forget, we are not just talking about monetary assets and liabilities. If you have a good deal of knowledge about a particular field of business you are about to enter, this should be counted as one of your most valuable assets. And vice versa—no experience is a negative point.

MANAGE WITH A PLAN

Many tasks, when you look at them the first time, appear to be so complex or so large as to be overwhelming. This is a normal reaction but it doesn't have to prevent you from accomplishing important objectives in life. Each problem you face is really a collection of smaller, simpler problems. The way to solve an unmanageable problem is to break it down into manageable segments and work on each one individually. Starting a new business is a tremendous undertaking and the complexity of it will often lead to a paralyzing sense of inadequacy unless you break the task down into several parts and then develop a written plan of action and a written timetable for accomplishing each portion of the business start up. Once you have the plan down on paper and see the first mini-problem resolved, you will feel the anxiety of inadequacy begin to melt away. This method is so effective that you will want to keep it in mind for later use when you begin other large projects in your business enterprise. Each problem solving plan must be adapted to the specific developmental phase of the project at hand; in other words, there may be plans within the plan. Right now you should be concerned with an overall strategy for handling the various projects necessary to get your new business off the ground. You want to devise a master plan into which all the subplans will fit as they are developed.

A master plan is not normally concerned with details. It should provide broad principles of organization, directions and means of action, and an appropriate timeframe for implementation. Specific undertakings, such as building a facility for your new business to function in may then be worked out in detail and inserted into the master plan.

Think your business plan out carefully and then stick to it as religiously as possible. There is no sense in developing an outline for your business progress if it is whimsically altered for the slightest reason. Of course your plans may require some changes to meet unforeseen circumstances but the changes should originate from a previously conceived method of integrating new data into your original plan.

QUANTIFY PLANNING WHENEVER POSSIBLE

At some point it will be necessary to begin planning the individual aspects of your horticultural business in greater detail. Depending upon the subject, some plans will be more adaptable to numerical representation and analysis than are others. If you are planning a greenhouse facility it is quite easy to arrive at a fairly exact cost estimate since the prices of various components are readily available. Such things as the relative merits of different plant varieties are more difficult to express in a numerical format because they are generally described with only words and phrases. It is possible, however, to assign numerical values to various plant characteristics and thereby rank different varieties in a quantitative fashion. You could then devise a crop plan which allowed you to choose between different varieties by comparing the numerical values assigned to them.

You must be the judge as to when a quantitative analysis of various problems is possible or justifiable. Some situations are simply not easily expressed in numerical terms with any degree of precision. I am not of the opinion that it is useful to quantify every aspect of your decision making process but I am suggesting that a strong reliance upon numerical expression in appropriate circumstances will lead you towards more satisfactory solutions. Numbers are more precise than words and hence, less subject to multiple interpretations. There is an old business adage which says "the numbers don't lie."

Sure it is hard work to slog through a financial statement, tediously certifying and inserting, in monetary terms, each detail of your material life. But the end result is more precise than simply saying "I feel rich" or "I feel poor." And the bottom line of a financial statement represents only one of many benefits. With all your material assets neatly expressed in numerical form, you can evaluate the strengths and weaknesses in your financial life. Decisions can then be initiated which will correct any imbalances.

Monetary information is not the only data which is expressed in an exact numerical format. If you are growing crops in the greenhouse or field, you can draw up a complete mathematical outline of what space crops will occupy throughout their growth, the quantity of different materials they will need for production, how many you plan to sell at

An example of data which can help in making business decisions. This is the first page of a two page financial statement.

different times, and so on. All of this numerical data can be used as an aid in crop scheduling and to produce a rather accurate estimate of crop profitability. An example of this process will be presented in a later chapter dealing with greenhouse crops.

Quantitative data is useful for your own planning and it is an absolute necessity when dealing with financial institutions and agencies. They simply will not talk with you about loans or grants without seeing a well thought out financial and business plan. Generally, the more numbers you give them, the happier they are.

EVALUATE BUSINESS PROPOSITIONS CAREFULLY

In the process of choosing a field of horticulture in which to do business you will likely encounter several ready made propositions which offer to get you started in a business venture without much work or knowledge on your part. The only way to separate the wheat from the chaff is to investigate any proposition carefully and logically. Don't believe any unsubstantiated claims which, upon reflection, do not make sense.

Certainly you do not want to discount all business propositions just because they did not originate as your own idea or because they propose to offer you knowledge and services for a fee. Some of the greatest business successes of postwar decades have been built upon such a concept; this is the franchise concept. But before you turn loose of any hard earned cash, make sure the proposition is reputable by checking out the background of the offering parties and by demanding references from existing customers.

I have only one further comment about prepackaged business propositions. The offering parties might be reputable and have previous customers who are happy and prosperous; but the deal simply may not be applicable to your circumstances. Standardized success formulas do not work in every case. Only you can be the judge!

Part II

MONEY MAKING
BUSINESSES
IN HORTICULTURE

This section will outline some money making horticultural businesses which might strike your interest. The main object is to let you know the variety of opportunities available, not to provide detailed operational plans for any particular enterprise. There are some limitations to my presentations because no one could be an expert in all aspects of any particular horticultural field, much less in all the fields to be touched upon. I have been exposed to numerous aspects of the horticultural industry over the years but my greatest personal experience is in the greenhouse area. No doubt you will find that, due to this reason, it is perhaps more completely covered than other topics.

Another reason I have limited my discussion of various fields is that I feel they offer potential only in a limited range of circumstances. Obviously, greenhouse and nursery production, and horticultural retailing are well developed in most parts of the country because there is a broad demand for these products and services. It makes sense to devote most of our attention to these topics because there is opportunity in almost every neighborhood. Success in some more specialized horticultural businesses may only be possible under specific circumstances of geography, climate, population, or other conditions.

Any presentation where numerous fields are considered must of course be greatly generalized. If you become especially interested in any specific horticultural area, you should realize the need to acquire a good deal more information about it than is presented in the following pages.

Chapter 4

PRODUCTION AND MARKETING OF GREENHOUSE ORNAMENTALS

Production of ornamentals under some type of protective structure is nothing new. Even ancient cultures engaged in this practice as early as suitable building materials became available. Until fairly recent times, however, most greenhouses were constructed for the private use of well to do individuals. Perhaps only in the past 200 years has there developed a serious commercial aspect to this age old preoccupation. Most growth in the industry has taken place since the beginning of the 20th century. The pace of construction, production, and demand seems to currently be expanding at an ever increasing rate.

It is hard to know whether the fevered pace is fueled by new construction and production technology which allows greenhouse growing to be done more easily and economically or if the increasing appreciation of ornamentals by affluent societies is the driving force. Whatever the case, this industry is booming without letup in sight.

The term greenhouse will be rather loosely used in this discussion. The average person in the northern United States likely envisions a greenhouse as being a structure covered by glass or perhaps some type of plastic-like material.

I believe we can continue to use this word profitably if we qualify it somewhat.

Well maintained greenhouses covered predominantly with fiberglass. This type of construction is intermediate in initial cost.

Inside a low cost polyethylene covered greenhouse which serves admirably for tropical foliage and seedling production despite the fact it is located in a near arctic climate.

The rigid, double layer plasticized panels used to cover this greenhouse cost a good deal more than fiberglass or polyethylene. This house was first covered over 50 years ago with glass. Notice the extensive use of large fans for exhausting warm air.

The most important qualification we must recognize is that much of what we might term greenhouse crop production now takes place outside of a traditional greenhouse structure. That is, production may occur in the open air or in shade structures near the greenhouse. This situation arose partially because optimum use of greenhouse space in some circumstances is accomplished if plants are stored in vertical layers in the structure at night and during inclement weather and then spread outside in daytime when weather permits. Another contributing reason is that much greenhouse production has shifted to the sunbelt states where it is possible to grow some crops, or at least some phases of crops, outdoors; often protected from the full sun by shade structures.

There are many commercial operations where it is difficult to decide whether they should be properly called greenhouses or nurseries. I suppose the deciding factor in most people's minds is whether the majority of crop production takes place inside, as in a greenhouse, or whether it predominantly takes place outdoors, as in a nursery. Also I believe most people associate the word nursery with woody ornamental production. There should be no great argument with using the terms somewhat interchangeably, as long as we become more precise whenever the need arises.

GREENHOUSES ALLOW CONTROLLED PRODUCTION

The main objectives of greenhouse production are generally to grow plants out of their normal season or habitat and in a more or less strictly controlled environment. The degree of environmental manipulation required to meet these objectives usually means that greenhouse crop culture is a rather costly alternative to open air field production. When the proper crops are chosen for greenhouse production and suitable markets are present, the grower hopefully will realize a profit which more than compensates for the additional costs involved in this type of intensive crop culture.

The progress of agriculture and industry in the modern world has generally been brought about by newer, more controlled methods of doing things. We have found that controlling natural processes usually results in increased efficiency and a greater total amount of desired product being available than is possible by simply letting nature take its course. This intensification and control of natural processes does not result without effort. Both resources and knowledge must be applied to make it work.

Since greenhouse culture requires the most precise environmental control of any widely used means of crop production, we might assume that it requires the most intensive use of both knowledge and resources. This is, in fact, the case. The practical impact of this situation is that, on average and for an equivalent business size, more monetary resources and technical background is required in the greenhouse production field than in most other aspects of horticulture.

ADVANTAGEOUS ASPECTS OF GREENHOUSE CULTURE

In return for the expenditure of considerable mental and monetary capital the greenhouse operator expects to realize definite commercial benefits. The most obvious advantage is that the grower can produce crops out of natural season at a time when they are in high demand. Other important advantages of greenhouse production over outdoor culture are: 1) predictable as well as accelerated production schedules are possible through control of temperature or other factors, and 2) physical protection of the crop from devastating climatic conditions is accomplished.

The advantages of greenhouse production over hit or miss open air methods intensify as our markets become more fine tuned and sophisticated. Often, consumers want their desires for horticultural products gratified whenever the urge hits them, not only when a product is in season. And in order to satisfy the market, distributors and retailers of ornamentals must demand a steady and reliable source of supply. They do not wish to have their marketing plans upset by frosts, windstorms, or drought conditions. In response to these market forces there has been a steady trend toward plant culture under cover.

Even in cases where a reasonably adequate outdoor growing program has traditionally been in place, many producers are now moving inside. A case in point is the Northwest Coast azalea production area. Years ago production was accomplished almost entirely outdoors during seasons which were not subject to frost. Growers would take cuttings in early spring, grow plants actively through the summer, and then allow buds to condition in the cool fall weather for Christmas and Valentines Day forcing.

Since a florist quality azalea took about two years production time, some protection was required in order to

A beautiful crop of florist azaleas being grown in July. In earlier years these Oregon plants would be outside during the warmer months. Greenhouses provide more predictable growing conditions than can be expected outdoors.

overwinter small plants intended for next year's crop. But the majority of a plant's life was spent outdoors.

Two main factors caused this time honored production method to be altered. First, many growers decided to move under cover because the possibility of devastating freezes in the fall as plants were being conditioned for market was unacceptable. And second, moving into greenhouses allowed growers to aim their marketing at Easter and Mothers Day market periods in addition to only the earlier Christmas and Valentines selling times. Some growers now produce azaleas year around. Moving azalea production indoors has led to a much extended selling season and this in turn has resulted in an overall expansion of the azalea industry. Generally, the growers are now more profitable and more financially stable than they were under the old outdoor cultural scheme.

Incidentally, I think you can see that in the past azalea producers were mostly thought of as nurserymen while at present a great number would be classified as greenhouse growers.

Another fact which emerges from this example is that most horticultural growers would be well advised to become familiar with greenhouse methods and techniques. Almost every crop requires some type of protected care during at least part of its life cycle.

HIGH INVESTMENT REQUIRES INTENSIVE MANAGEMENT

The monetary investment required to build greenhouses varies dramatically from structure to structure, depending upon materials, labor, and the degree of environmental control necessary. If you build a bare bones structure with your own labor and use second hand materials, the actual cash expenses for a greenhouse may be very small. But a brand new structure which will handle all climatic conditions the year around can be quite expensive, especially if a contractor builds the greenhouse for you.

In order to recoup your investment you must manage a greenhouse intensively. You can't let it sit half empty when it should be full of plants. And the crops you produce must be of high enough quality to bring a profitable price. The more you invest in a greenhouse the more intensively it must be utilized. Greenhouse managers generally measure crop productivity in terms of how many square feet a crop occupies for a specific period of time. In 1992 it costs the average commercial greenhouse owner approximately $0.10 to $0.20 per square foot per week to cover operational and structure expenses only. This figure does not cover materials such as seed, soil, starter plants, or other costs directly attributable to a specific crop. Thus, a 2000 square foot greenhouse (small by industry standards) would be costing $200.00 to $400.00 per week just to keep operational. Of course if you build an inexpensive greenhouse on surplus land and operate it yourself, you can lower these costs a great deal.

The point is, an empty or inefficiently managed greenhouse is costing you money, not making money. Many greenhouses are constructed and managed only for spring operation. This is okay as long as the owner builds inexpensive structures and slashes operational expenses as soon as the crop is out the door. In fact, this is one of the better operational methods for newcomers in the business to use. But if you build an expensive greenhouse and provide heat and staff all winter, it must be filled with marketable crops.

THE GREENHOUSE CROP PLAN

The controlled environment in greenhouses allows growers in Maine to produce more or less the same crops as could be grown in a Texas greenhouse. Thus, the cultural details for specific crops are fairly uniform from region to region. Why is it then, that upon visiting a number of greenhouses one finds that each establishment has developed its own special style or method of operation? And why will each owner or manager usually swear that their method is the right one?

You must realize that although greenhouses are intended to modify the natural climatic conditions, each increased degree of climatic modification normally involves an increase in operational cost.

Therefore, some of the restraints of the natural climate usually still apply to greenhouse production. And they apply in differing degrees depending upon the construction characteristics of each particular greenhouse.

Climate and differences in greenhouse construction are not the only causes of diversity in operational methods. Hundreds of potential crops are available for culture under greenhouse conditions. The grower must determine which crops are most profitably adapted to the particular conditions prevailing for production and marketing. There are numerous technical and economic reasons why a grower might select one crop over another: 1) the proper raw materials for good growth may not be economically available, 2) growers may lack enough knowledge or information, 3) certain crops may be subject to disease or insect predation, 4) one crop may require more energy input than another, 5) and on and on. But the most important factor determining the crops a producer should grow is what ones can actually be sold at a healthy profit.

Marketing possibilities vary from region to region and even from neighborhood to neighborhood, thus causing greenhouse operators to choose a variety of production scenarios, each hopefully resulting in a successful outcome for the business involved.

However variable the crop production plans are among individual greenhouses, there do arise some general patterns within the industry.

In other words, many greenhouses share a relatively common production schedule in regards to the timing and species of crops grown while other growers concentrate their efforts upon somewhat different production schemes. These differences and similarities arise in response to the factors mentioned above which influence the decisions of individual growers. Basically, many growers make the same decisions so that we see general patterns arise among their operational plans.

I will now outline a few of the more common production scenarios into which greenhouses may be classified. Remember that seldom would you find a facility which epitomized these descriptions perfectly, some degree of hybridization between plans is almost always the case.

Garden season only operation

This method of ornamental crop production is quite common amongst beginning and part time growers in all sections of the country. It is also popular with more established full time growers in climates where active gardening is practiced throughout a large part of the year. Needless to say, the crops grown are those which consumers use in their gardening.

Garden plants of all types have become big business over the last twenty years; and it is this segment of the greenhouse industry which is booming the most. A voracious and generally profitable market is the main reason why so many growers gravitate towards production of garden plants. There are, however, other reasons which influence their decision: 1) relatively inexpensive structures are needed, 2) the manager or owner can be free other parts of the year to pursue alternative interests, 3) money is tied up only a short time in supplies and expenses, and 4) the degree of technical expertise required is relatively limited.

The growing climate inside and outside the greenhouse at the time garden plants are being cropped is generally pleasant and relatively problem free. Hard to manage extremes of light and temperature associated with winter and mid summer production are avoided for the most part when an operation concentrates on garden plants.

Of course the big drawback in this type of operation is the lack of cash flow during the remaining part of the year. It seems a shame to build greenhouses and then shut them down after only a relatively short period of operation.

But remember! Our goal is profit. If market and production conditions outside the gardening season are not amenable to profitable operation, be happy with what you can get and leave the money losing work to someone else. Several of the most monetarily successful and happy greenhouse owners I know have concentrated strictly upon garden plants and are content to be on vacation the rest of the year.

Most greenhouses get all the business they can handle during the spring rush but the trick is to provide product and convince consumers to buy it a month or two on either side of the busy season. Granted, the amount of business you generate at these times may not be fantastic but if the rush season covers your expenses and provides a small profit, the extra sales early and late are pure gravy. There are several strategies you can use to increase the length of time garden plants or associated products can be sold profitably.

During the pre season, you might concentrate upon seeds, planting supplies, and cold hardy plants. And since there will be many gardeners at this time seeking a project they can accomplish indoors, it is wise to have inexpensive and appealing houseplants available as impulse items. Even small tomato plants will sell reasonably well because early

Early season planting supplies and fertilizer can help start the cash coming in before customers are interested in flowering plants for the garden.

bird gardeners want to grow them even larger before the time to plant outside arrives.

After the main busy season, full bloom hanging baskets and patio planters sell very well if you provide a quality product at a reasonable price. The secret to late season sales is in growing fresh crops specifically designed for this market period. People don't want your left over plants from the rush

Beautiful patio planters like this can help extend the selling season in a greenhouse by at least one month. They also allow customers to visualize what the smaller plants they buy will look like later.

season. And at the very end of the season, when you think no one would buy another plant, a half price sale of first rate merchandise will prolong the season for another two or three weeks.

Although I operate my greenhouse business year around, the spring season in 1991 accounted for 90 percent of profits. At one time the wintertime business in ornamental plants and flowers was very good in our locale, but a severe economic depression in the region's main industries has prompted consumers to limit their purchases of luxury items. Happily, the amount of spring business remains steady and I have been able to modify my operation so as to take full advantage of our short gardening season. My business is still prospering while others have long since fallen prey to the poor economy.

I have emphasized the gardening season only scheme of greenhouse operation because it is likely to be the first step many of you take towards a career in specialized horticulture. There is a tremendous demand for garden plants in every neighborhood. Even urban dwellers are now eager buyers of plant products designed for limited space gardening. A beginner in the spring greenhouse business can easily sell a large amount of plants at retail prices even if only the basics of an intelligent marketing plan are followed. With hard work and careful advance planning, it is possible to realize a full year's profits with only a four or five month operation.

One basic problem which the spring only grower faces is the task of finding competent employees who are willing and able to work only a few months of the year. This drawback is not usually serious for the smaller grower who can rely upon neighborhood housewives and afterschool teenagers to fill the gap. But it is a major handicap for those who wish to expand this type of business beyond the possibilities of a small retail greenhouse. So although a spring only greenhouse can be very profitable as a start up enterprise, the limitation it imposes upon the development of a trained labor force for future expansion must be clearly recognized.

Combining garden season plants and holiday flowers

Most greenhouse growers get their start producing bedding plants for the gardening market. As they gain more experience and if they want to be in the greenhouse business year around, they begin to look for ways to utilize their greenhouses longer during the year.

A large number of these people settle into a production scheme which emphasizes garden plants during the season and then switches to flowering pot plants from fall through midwinter. Poinsettias for Christmas are usually the main money making flower crop in this type of operation but Thanksgiving, Valentines Day, and Easter, in increasing order of importance can also be relied upon to provide a market for potted flowers. At Mother's Day, which is perhaps the largest flower occasion of the year, growers are faced with a conflict between space needed by spring garden crops and space for potted flowers.

A cropping scheme like this can significantly increase income and also allow key employees to remain at work all year. The drawbacks are that better structures are needed for winter production and a higher and more varied level of knowledge on the part of the grower is required. In addition, most growers have a hard time selling all the potted flowers they can grow at a retail price. They must usually sell a large proportion of these flowers at wholesale to flower shops and mass outlets. Thus, except in the best circumstances, winter flower production is seldom as profitable as is spring garden plant production. And in contrast to the vigorous growth plants exhibit in the spring, winter culture is sometimes difficult with large amounts of heat usually being needed to force plants along. I do not wish to discourage anyone by my cautionary statements from planning a year round commercial greenhouse. But I must point out that it is a more complex and risky venture than is an in and out spring only operation. If you expect to expand beyond the limitations of a small neighborhood greenhouse it is almost obligatory that you progress beyond growing strictly spring crops.

Continuous foliage plant and potted flower production

Although the garden plant market is generally the most profitable aspect of greenhouse production, some growers find that over the long run, a cultural scheme which leads to a steady flow of plant production through the year is best suited to their facilities, markets, and personal inclination. This objective is often accomplished by specializing in indoor foliage plants and decorative potted flowers. Individual greenhouses may specialize in only foliage, only potted flowers, or both at the same time.

If you have a large retail outlet or multiple outlets, it is possible to market a good deal of foliage and flowers by this means. But most growers in this production scheme find that they cannot move a large enough volume through their own retail efforts to support a year round growing operation. They must then look to other florists and mass outlets as buyers for their excess production.

Some greenhouses, either from the start or in a step by step progression, become totally oriented toward wholesale production of foliage, potted flowers, or both. Needless to say, the wholesale operations must be of considerable size to generate enough volume so that adequate total profit is realized. Wholesale profit margins simply do not lead to a good income picture unless large amounts of merchandise are sold. This is the basic premise of the wholesale trade— large volume at low price.

Beginners in the greenhouse business must not allow themselves to be drawn into impossible situations. A small neighborhood greenhouse operated solely by the owner cannot produce enough plants economically to compete in the wholesale area unless special circumstances apply. Yes, it may be possible to sell all that you produce at a fair market price but unless you grow a large volume of plants efficiently, the wholesale price you receive will not cover production expenses. A small greenhouse must generally operate on retail terms to be successful.

The statements I have just made about wholesale business are based solely upon strict accounting procedures. It may well be that if every expense is not accounted for you may find yourself ahead monetarily every year. That is to say, if you do not charge the cost of land, taxes, minor utilities, some family labor, and miscellaneous expenses against the business it may appear that a profit is being made. This is a common mistake of people whose personal assets are unavoidably mixed with a business operation. They let the business use their personal assets for free. The only way to see if a true business profit is being made is to charge the business for all materials and services you provide to it.

A steady, repetitive cropping system throughout the year and from year to year allows growers to plan production and marketing carefully and fine tune their efficiency. If you must seek outside financing, this is the type of predictable and stable situation which loan officials will look upon most favorably—even if it may not yield the greatest profits. And some growers prefer the reduced anxiety and risk levels which result from a repetitive schedule.

Of course if you can't sell all your production at retail, then there is the problem of contacting and convincing other retail outlets to handle your plants and flowers. This is not usually an easy task in the beginning but fortunately it becomes almost automatic after accounts have been established. As long as you provide good merchandise and service at a fair price!

The best way to get established in a steady flower and foliage production scheme is to ease into it gradually over several years. Seldom will a grower have enough technical and marketing expertise to start a profitable year round operation from scratch. Most likely you will want to start a seasonal spring operation, then graduate to producing a few holiday potted flowers in conjunction with spring plants, and then (if it seems advisable) begin aiming at specializing in year around flowers and foliage.

Single crop specialist

As a grower becomes established in a greenhouse operation, it sometimes becomes apparent that the most satisfactory course for future expansion lies in producing a single specialized crop. The factors causing this situation may vary but in many cases, it results from a consuming interest which the grower develops in a particular group of plants. Other major factors can be market conditions and local climatic suitability.

This type of operation usually sells crops on the wholesale market and, as a result, must be of sufficient size to produce enough volume for satisfactory profits. Sometimes the specialized plants being grown require extraordinary facilities and technical knowledge, this fact may protect the grower from widespread competition and allow for a highly profitable situation even with a limited volume of crops. The latter situation does not occur often or endure for extended periods because it is usually only a matter of time before the necessary knowledge becomes widespread. Basing a business upon a single product allows for the concentration of energy and capital in a very efficient manner. However, this is a two edged sword. A single product company is vulnerable to factors which make the product obsolete.

A perfect example of this situation is the carnation industry in Colorado. Until the 1950's, Colorado was the carnation capital of America but as jet air cargo became both efficient and reliable, cut flowers could be economically shipped from continent to continent. Because the higher altitudes of Colombia, South America were even more suitable to carnation growing than was Colorado and because labor was cheaper in Colombia, large carnation growers established production facilities there and Colorado was eclipsed as a major force in carnation production. Most Colorado carnation growers went broke or switched to other crops.

Specialization in plant products not widely available from other sources is a proven route to success in the greenhouse industry.

There are several crops in which growers seem to have specialized for one reason or another. The driving forces are complex and not appropriate for investigation in an introductory book but the fact is that specialization is one of several proven routes to success in the greenhouse industry. Growers of azaleas, cactus, bromeliads, bonsai trees, roses, and several other major and minor crops are more often than not, specialists in only that crop.

If you possess specialized knowledge about a group of economically valuable or potentially valuable ornamental plants, it may well be that a specialized greenhouse operation would suit you fine. More than one individual has become rich and famous by developing their interest in a particular group of plants into a successful business enterprise.

Starter plant specialist

In the early stages of life plants, like humans, are in special need of intensive and constant care. Whether they receive adequate nurture during juvenile stages often determines their productivity as adult specimens. This intensive care is best accomplished in special facilities where a higher level of supervision and technical knowledge is available.

Many experienced greenhouse growers who possess the resources, both mentally and monetarily, to provide intensive care conditions have specialized as producers of starter plants for the rest of the industry. Often these growers will also be engaged in developing new varieties for which they obtain government patents. As the owner of a patented variety you are allowed by law to control the reproduction of the variety in question. You may restrict propagation to your own facilities or license other growers to reproduce the plants, for which they pay a royalty fee.

The more successful propagation specialists are often considered leaders in the industry since a large number of unspecialized and smaller growers are dependent upon the specialist as a source for healthy starter plants and for cultural information. Many propagation specialists amass considerable wealth since other growers are willing to pay a handsome price in order to avoid the headaches of starting their own plants.

If a specialist happens to develop and patent a particularly popular variety, it can be the horticultural equivalent of writing a best selling book or producing an academy award winning movie. A plant patent lasts for many years and even a modestly successful variety may be the source of considerable royalty income over an extended period of time.

Only a small number of propagation specialists ever attain "star" status but many become regional or local suppliers of starter plants of one or several varieties. Plant propagation is a process in which success depends heavily upon the practitioner's strict attention to detail and cleanliness. Anyone who is not disposed towards these attributes should forget about becoming a starter plant specialist.

Cut flower specialist

Cut flowers were at one time, probably the major crop in most greenhouses all across America. Now they are of major importance only in specific areas and with a limited number of growers. Although their numbers have decreased, the average size of cut flower greenhouse ranges and the total production of cut flowers has increased. This change has been brought about by the general tendency of business in America towards specialization and by changes in the transportation system.

Because they have been detached from the root ball, cut flowers are rather light in weight when compared to most other ornamental crops. And, because in most varieties the blooms can be laid flat on top of one another without significant damage, cut flowers are easily and economically shipped by air. As air freight services became dependable, widespread, and cheap it was more economical for cut flowers to be grown in areas where the climate was near ideal and labor cheap. The majority of cut flowers in the United States are now grown in California and Florida. A good deal of total production in some varieties is grown outside under field conditions. As was mentioned in the previous chapter, because air transport has become so economical, much of the cut flowers used in the United States are now produced overseas. Colombia, The Netherlands, Spain, Israel, and Australia are major suppliers.

The situation in cut flowers today does not lend itself to easy entry by small diversified growers. But there are isolated possibilities for local greenhouses to supply cut flowers under specific conditions. Some smaller growers concentrate upon varieties which can be shipped only with difficulty. Snapdragons are a case in point. The blooms do not pack well and, in addition, quality snapdragons are not easily grown under the warm weather conditions usually prevailing in the major cut flower growing regions. There are several minor cutflower crops in which the same or similar conditions prevail. So if you are a cut flower enthusiast, take heart, there is still room for you in the greenhouse industry but you must choose your crops and markets carefully to make a profit.

GREENHOUSES NOT SELF SUFFICIENT

No matter what type of cropping system your greenhouse may emphasize or where it is located, you will usually be dependent upon other greenhouses to supply some of your plant or flower needs. Seldom is a greenhouse 100% self sufficient as far as plant needs are concerned. Most purchase a fair amount of seedlings and rooted cuttings from specialists and some buy in a good amount of finished flowers and plants to round out their inventory.

There is nothing wrong with this situation as long as it is part of a well thought out production and marketing plan rather than resulting from laziness or a fear of overcoming specific crop culture problems. In fact, some greenhouse owners, after careful thought, find that buying most of their plants and merely using their greenhouse as an inventory holding area is the most efficient and profitable method of operation. The latter situation is not much different than being strictly a retail outlet, except that a larger backup of inventory is held in stock.

No one can prescribe how much plant material you should buy from other sources. It depends upon the prices and selection available, how good a grower you are, transport factors, and many other variables. But mostly it depends upon the marketing and cultural plan you have devised.

Under most circumstances, I favor being as independent as possible from outside suppliers of plant material. In this way you develop a completely integrated cultural and marketing system, which minimizes the probability of disruptions in your supply line. An example of the problems you can get into relying upon other growers is the common practice of buying geranium cuttings from outside sources for the spring crop. If the supplying grower does not ship your cuttings or gets them to you a month late, you miss the peak selling season for one of your most important crops. And believe me, this scenario is not rare!

Another big reason I favor being relatively independent is the difficulty a lot of small town growers have getting plant material delivered safely and economically to their locale. Besides, doesn't it seem as if you could raise the product at a slightly higher cost than the other grower and then pocket at least some of the freight money?

There are certainly times and situations when you should buy in plant material, but weigh the alternatives carefully. The expenses can mount up quickly and suck most of the profit out of your operation. Isolated small town growers must be especially willing to remain self sufficient.

EXAMPLE OF GREENHOUSE EXPENSES AND PROFITS

Although each greenhouse operation will have a somewhat different economic picture, I think it will be beneficial to examine a specific example in detail. This will not only give you actual figures for a common cropping scheme but it will familiarize you with a method by which other greenhouse crops may be analyzed. The method could also be used, with minor modifications, for examining the economics involved with other horticultural business enterprises which will be described later in this book.

Inside a greenhouse of the type and approximate size specified for our cost analysis presented in the text. Low cost but very sturdy and modern.

The example I will present involves a small greenhouse of 3000 square feet which is to be operated only in the spring. I portray this situation because it is a fairly common size greenhouse and cropping scheme for a newcomer in the industry to select. Normally this size greenhouse will not produce adequate income to support a family but it is a good size to start out with part time the first year. I would say that about 9000 square feet of greenhouse space is necessary to realize a good family income if the operation sells its produce mainly at retail and most labor is provided by family members. There are several qualifications which we must place upon the example to be examined in order to interpret it accurately. The qualifications are presented in Table 2.

Table 2

Qualifying statements which apply to Tables 3 and 4 of the greenhouse economic model which follows.

A. Greenhouse structure is of new material and adequately equipped to operate in spring and fall of a moderately cold climate.

B. Owner supplies labor to build greenhouse except for a few specific tasks, such as electrical hookups and occasional hourly labor hired.

C. Owner supplies land and utility access.

D. Greenhouse structure is an engineered steel frame, double inflated plastic kit available from manufacturers and is of modern design with automatic heat, cooling fans, and inflation blowers.

E. Owner devotes approximately 1000 hours per year to growing and selling spring crop, making repairs, record keeping and planning.

F. Model assumes one complete crop of standard spring bedding plants in flats, each flat occupying 1.5 square feet and containing 12 packs of 6 plants each. This equals a total of 2,000 flats each year.

G. Hanging baskets overhead in greenhouse will replace the value of any bedding flats accounted for in model but not actually grown because some space is necessary for aisles.

H. With a 3% dumpage rate the number of flats available for sale is reduced to 1,940 per year.

I. Retail price of $20.28 per flat is actual price obtained by author's retail department in 1992. This is higher than average chain store prices but lower than some independent garden center prices.

J. Assume plants will be sold retail at the greenhouse. If alternative lot space in high traffic area is rented for retail sales, the $2000.00 budgeted for advertising would be used for spring season rental.

K. Building and related equipment costs are taken from actual 1992 catalog prices while miscellaneous construction costs are estimated from author's experience. Fixed greenhouse operation costs are estimated from author's experience while variable product costs per unit are taken from author's own production cost records in commercial greenhouse.

Table 3

Expenses involved in operating a 3,000 square foot commercial greenhouse for the spring gardening season only. These costs can be lowered by using recycled pots, used equipment, and doing more work yourself.

Building and equipment costs—assume new steel frame prefabricated greenhouse kit is purchased.

Greenhouse kit with frame, endwalls, doors	$2700.00
Heater, ventilation fan, water lines, and utility hookups	3200.00
Ground preparation and concrete for posts	600.00
Wheel barrow, pump, soil mixer, miscellaneous equipment. Used condition if possible	1100.00
Total building and equipment costs	7600.00
Yearly building and equipment cost if total is amortized at 12% interest over a 15 year usable lifespan	1094.64

Variable product costs per unit of plants produced

Containers for plants	$0.25
Flats—used only 1 year	0.35
Soil	0.25
Seed and germination materials	1.00
Total variable cost per unit (flat)	1.85

Fixed greenhouse operation costs per year

Yearly cost for double layer polyethylene covering on greenhouse if replaced 4 times in a 15 year period . .	$150.00
Insurance	500.00
Water	400.00
Heating fuel	1100.00
Electricity	300.00
Fertilizer	200.00
Pest control	200.00
Maintenance and repair materials	500.00
Taxes, property	300.00
Miscellaneous expenses	500.00
Total fixed operating costs	4150.00

Table 4

Revenues, costs, and profits for operating a 3000 square foot greenhouse in spring gardening season only. Refer to Table 2 for qualifying statements.

Calculation of yearly revenues

Greenhouse produces 1 spring crop for a total of 2,000 flats.
Multiply this by a retail selling price of $20.28 per
flat to arrive at total gross revenues $40560.00

Calculation of yearly selling and production costs

Cost of advertising or high traffic sales lot rental to
reach customers, assume 5% of gross revenues
(0.05 x $40560.00) $2028.00
Extra sales help in busiest month at $6.00 per hour . . . 1000.00
Deduct for 3% crop spoilage (0.03 x 40560.00) 1216.80
Variable cost of planting 2,000 flats of plants
at $1.85 each 3700.00
Fixed operating costs per year from Table 3 . . . . 4150.00
Building and equipment costs per year from Table 3 . . 1094.64
Total costs per year for selling and production 13189.44

Calculation of before tax profits

Total retail revenues less total production and selling
costs ($40560.00 - $13189.44) $27370.56

The descriptive terms and numerical information given in Tables 2,3, and 4 will require a few minutes of study in order to completely understand what they mean. I am trying to accurately show you how much it would cost to build and operate a greenhouse through the spring gardening season. When all expenses are subtracted from gross revenues (sales) we arrive at a before tax profit.

There are several points which may require some clarification. First, the profit figure represents what you could expect for devoting approximately 1/2 of a normal work year to the greenhouse enterprise.

A 40 hour work week equals 2080 hours a year while our example requires you to put in only 1000 hours. Of course, if you wanted to you could have someone to do most of this work. You should double the profit figure to arrive at a fair estimate of how much you would make if you devoted full time to the greenhouse.

The greenhouse structure should have a usable lifespan of at least 15 years. I am adding to yearly expenses only the annual mortgage payment (taken from bank mortgage tables) necessary to pay off the greenhouse completely in 15 years. The entire greenhouse cost cannot be attributed to a single year, it must be spread out evenly over its 15 year lifespan.

The term "flats" in our example may be unfamiliar to some readers. It is a trade term which means the outer tray into which the growing containers are placed. We have based our example calculations upon plants being grown only in this type of container. In reality you would likely grow in several different container sizes and types but the price you would receive per square foot of space occupied would at least equal the price received per square foot occupied by "flats". In my experience, the relative retail price of plants in flats is less than plants in other size containers. I have made this simplication to make the example more easily understood.

The $27370.56 profit figure for half time work may not impress some of you who already make a lot of money but it is a significant income for many people. You also have the option (for very little extra construction expense) of equipping the greenhouse to produce crops all year. And you should realize that if you expand your operation to 4 or 5 or even 10 of these greenhouses, you could easily manage them by yourself with a few lower level employees.

I expect that the price I receive for my plants (which is used in the example) can at least be matched by other growers. My prices are on the upper end but certainly not the highest in town. Total income can be increased by selling such things as seed, fertilizers, potting soil, and other related products which complement the greenhouse plants.

Many of you are probably thinking now that you would like to get into a greenhouse business but cannot see any way to come up with the $10000.00 - $15000.00 investment necessary to build and operate the greenhouse used in the example. I will address this concern in a later chapter of this book. At the present time I will only say that there are many financing alternatives possible, especially if you own a piece of land or a home. The easiest way to cut start up costs is by building your own greenhouse from scrap materials and by cutting a few corners with equipment, heaters, and other materials.

These elementary figures demonstrate that there are good financial opportunities in the horticultural field. The satisfaction of being your own boss and the healthy mix of mental and physical work are added psychological benefits you may enjoy. I feel growing and selling plants is a very secure occupation. As the pressures of modern living increase, more people turn to decorating with plants indoors and gardening to alleviate their tensions. The trend toward urbanized societies means these pressures will grow even more and thus ensure a healthy market for plants and flowers in the future.

Most of the really successful greenhouse owners I know started their enterprise as a sideline while they worked at regular jobs. After a year or two of learning the ropes and developing a clientele they usually saw their businesses take off at an astounding rate. There are numerous extremely large greenhouse firms started only a few years ago by individuals like you. The horticultural industry is truly in a boom era and will stay that way as long as the trends of the last twenty years continue. Sales of foliage plants, potted flowers, and bedding plants have increased greatly in recent years. There is plenty of room in this expanding market for newcomers.

OUTLOOK FOR THE GREENHOUSE INDUSTRY

In addition to the generally rosy economic outlook for greenhouse products, there are some specific points I would like to consider which relate fundamentally to the greenhouse physical environment.

Climate inside the greenhouse can be altered so that a particular crop may be grown under ideal conditions in almost any geographical setting.

This situation assures that new or improved ornamental plant varieties can and will be grown in any region of the world where profitable consumer markets exist. Development of these new varieties in response to market demand will lead to a continual stream of new ornamental plant products. This is a very healthy condition for the greenhouse industry. We have new and exciting products each year to help expand sales.

The greenhouse climate also assures that we have a drawing card to attract production workers at reasonable wages. Other industries and other segments of the horticultural industry are not so lucky. A large number of people consider greenhouse work to be a pleasant indoor job. The same cannot be said of an outdoor ornamental nursery where plants are generally many times larger and the weather often unfavorable. So the greenhouse industry has an inside track on one of the most important problems facing American business—how to attract and hold competent workers at reasonable prices.

The explosion of technical knowledge in the greenhouse industry has only just begun and indicates that we may expect the culture of ornamentals under cover to continue expanding significantly for many years.

Chapter 5

PRODUCTION AND MARKETING OF ORNAMENTAL NURSERY PLANTS GROWN OUTDOORS

The distinction which I am making between greenhouse grown and outdoor grown ornamentals in this book is not entirely satisfactory since there are all sorts of situations where the dividing line becomes fuzzy. Some plants are grown indoors for awhile and then finished outside; or certain crops may be moved in and out, depending upon the weather. But I think the distinction generally has some usefulness and I hope you will be helped more than you are confused by my method of presentation.

In the previous chapter we listed the several advantages of greenhouse culture over outdoor production and there is no need to explore this topic in greater detail. It will be enough to emphasize again that the chief reason most production still occurs outside is that it is more economical for most varieties during the majority of their life cycle. An open field is less expensive to own and operate than is a greenhouse.

Anyone who has time, knowledge, and a piece of ground can get started in the business of producing ornamental plants outdoors. A lack of capital and other amenities may limit the types and amounts of nursery stock you can grow but it does not prevent you from getting established in one form or another. Even if you don't own any land it is almost always possible to rent or lease a small parcel on very reasonable terms.

Many species of common nursery plants can be reproduced from seed, cuttings, or divisions which are free for the gathering in your immediate neighborhood. Getting started in the business needn't involve purchasing a lot of expensive starter plants from other growers. Buying plants helps you avoid the time consuming process of starting from scratch and it enables you to offer a broader line of merchandise but it runs up costs considerably. You must decide whether it is advisable to start most of your own small plants or buy them. If you have the resources, it will likely prove most effective to buy all varieties except those which are easiest to start. Many of the newer tree varieties are propagated by grafting techniques which are not economical for smaller growers to practice.

MANAGE NURSERY OPERATIONS EFFECTIVELY

It may appear that since nursery land is relatively cheap, when compared to a greenhouse structure, the manager or owner of an outdoor nursery could enjoy a somewhat more relaxed approach toward business. This may be true to a certain extent, but in some respects, the nurseryman's life is more difficult because outdoor crops are subject to many perils not present in the controlled greenhouse climate. And the most difficult job—that of selling the crop profitably is no less a challenge to the outdoor producer.

Although the outdoor ornamental plant grower may have less initial monetary investment to lose in case of business failure, the enterprise must still be managed intensively and effectively in order to develop a profitable operation. Just because there is little risk of losing a good deal of money doesn't mean that profits will magically appear. And it is sometimes harder for people to maintain the necessary degree of vigilance and motivation if they are not subject to a high risk level.

Typical outdoor shade structure used to offer some protection for nursery crops. Can be used as a selling area, as in this photograph, or as a nurse area for newly potted stock.

Each step of your nursery growing operation must be carefully coordinated with a definite marketing program before you set out the first row of trees or shrubs. The most serious business mistake a nursery grower is liable to make is that of growing crops helter skelter without a timetable, cultural plan, or a well conceived means of selling the crop. Remember, you are in business—not dabbling at a hobby!

NURSERY OWNERS MUST BE PATIENT

Traditionally, nursery owners have measured crop cycles in years rather than weeks or months. This type of schedule does not suit people who expect immediate results. Although the amount of time required to raise some types of nursery crops has been reduced through new growing methods, you must still be of a patient nature to thrive in this business.

The often slow growth progress of nursery crops means that you must plan ahead carefully to make sure your cultural and marketing plan results in the desired outcome after you have invested several years of effort in a crop.

Inventory turnover in some types of nursery operations can be very slow in the early years of business. If you are specializing in larger specimen trees of slower growing varieties, it could be five years or more before you harvest the first crop of saleable trees. An operation that is planned around varieties and plant sizes which offer a relatively quick inventory turnover will result in cash flow beginning the first year.

NURSERY PLANTS AND CLIMATE

Outdoor nursery production is primarily controlled by climatic conditions which exist at the site. Selling of crops is also dependent upon weather to a large degree. The unique character of each local climate, even from town to town, can work both to the benefit or detriment of nursery operations. If you are not careful, you will reap most of the disadvantages while gathering few of the benefits.

The plant varieties selected for cultivation and almost every aspect of their subsequent growth will in some way be dependent upon climatic conditions. Even the influence of ancient climates will be reflected in the materials composing field soils. Nursery managers must learn to accept the limits which climate places upon them, you cannot do battle with such powerful forces and expect to win. Of course there are some small tricks of the trade which can help overcome minor climatic hurdles but, by and large, your business is at the mercy of Mother Nature. Learn to live with her.

On the other side of the coin, climatic variability provides an opportunity for the smaller retail grower to attract and hold customers through his or her intimate knowledge of how to grow landscape plants successfully in the local area. This advantage may not be of great importance for larger wholesale growers who depend upon far away

THESE HARDY PERENNIALS HAVE BEEN GROWN OUTSIDE ALL WINTER. THEY CAN BE PLANTED DIRECTLY IN THE GROUND NOW.

WE RECOMMEND COVERING ONLY IF THE TEMPERATURE DROPS BELOW 25°.

Informational signs which let customers know about the benefits of buying locally produced plants will help you sell crops at top prices.

clients to purchase most of their product but it is the key element for success in the type of local retail nursery most readers of this book are likely to start.

Thus, one of the major disadvantages of outdoor crop culture can actually be turned into a competitive edge by those nursery people who exploit it fully. You must let customers know at every turn the benefits of purchasing trees and shrubs produced locally by a person who understands the cultural methods necessary for successful landscaping at their home or business. In fact, your knowledge should be the main commodity of business, with the plant material producing the initial point of contact between you and the customer. And you must be sure to set prices at levels which will adequately compensate for the valuable knowledge provided to customers.

You will always be faced with the challenge of discount stores selling nursery stock at prices which often do not even equal your costs of production. There is no way the independent nursery can compete pricewise, you must build a business upon knowledgeable advice and high levels of service to that segment of the consumer market which is willing to pay for what you offer. And apparently most people still prefer to buy their landscape plants from independent operators. Every reputable market survey released to this date shows that independent nurseries and garden centers remain the first choice of consumers for purchases of plant material.

Since climate affects nursery crop culture so dramatically, it is hardly surprising that finding books which outline the commercial culture of particular varieties are hard to find and seldom provide accurate information about growing under all the conditions which are likely to be encountered. It would be next to impossible for an author to deal with the thousands of nursery varieties popular in various sections of the United States, much less to provide cultural guides for production of each one under the varying climatic and soil conditions which might be present.

COMBINATION OF NURSERY AND LANDSCAPING BUSINESS

A complete landscaping and plant installation service is a logical extension of the specialized retail services you should offer at the nursery sales lot. In some cases nursery owners have found that the landscaping service is a more lucrative business proposition than is selling plants. Although a landscaping enterprise can be profitable in and of itself, the more successful ones are usually an offshoot of a nursery operation. Undoubtedly this is the case because being in the nursery business allows you to more easily carry a large inventory of plants for landscaping jobs and helps in making contacts with potential customers. Clients who see an established business in operation will feel more assured that the landscape job is guaranteed by a substantial firm.

FIELD AND CONTAINER NURSERIES

Until after World War II almost every nursery was a field operation which resembled a typical farm. The nurseries might be generally smaller and more intensively worked than were fields of agricultural crops but the basic operation was similar. And nursery stock was sold as bareroot material for immediate planting in the customer's yard or sometimes, especially with evergreens, as balled and burlapped stock which allowed customers some leeway as to when the plant could be placed in the landscape. The planting season was limited to the cooler times of year when plants could stand the shock of being transplanted.

This was an unfavorable situation for both the nursery owner and customers. The nursery owner wanted a method of production and marketing which would allow for a longer selling season and for less concentration of production activities in the spring months. Customers hoped for some means of being able to enjoy planting through the summer and of seeing their trees and shrubs leafed out and growing before sticking them in the ground.

It is surprising that the nursery industry took so long to come up with the concept of containerized nursery stock. Sure there were isolated growers who used this method of operation in earlier years but only since the 1950's has the containerized plant become the almost universally accepted means of offering nursery stock for sale at the retail level. And many producers have gone a step further by growing their plants in containers from start to finish. The container revolution has allowed nursery stock to be effectively marketed by mass merchandisers but it has also made it possible for independent retailers to actively sell healthy plants through most of the year. This has greatly increased their cash flow.

The field nursery

The preference of retail nursery outlets for containerized plant material might lead you to believe that most plants are now grown in containers. This is not the case. Field grown nursery stock still accounts for the majority of production; the major change being not in how the plants are grown initially but in how they are marketed to the final customer. Today most of the smaller trees and shrubs grown in fields are destined to be planted in containers before being sold at retail. Most larger field grown trees are still sold as balled and burlapped stock but there is, even here, some trend toward containerization.

Field growing has, to a large extent, ceased to be a major activity at most retail nurseries. The smaller retail nursery owner usually finds that it is more efficient to purchase the lion's share of plant material to be containerized from wholesale specialists. Many retail operations still maintain a limited field area for growing specialty crops which they consider economical or which they cannot easily find elsewhere.

Although the field grown nursery business is dominated by a relatively few large wholesale growers, there is room in this segment of the industry for new smaller growers who limit their activities to specialized high value crops and who supply landscapers and retail consumers with the convenience of locally grown material.

The container nursery

There are two general ways of operating a container growing operation for trees and shrubs. Either you buy bareroot or balled and burlapped stock from a specialist and pot it up shortly before sale or you actually grow the plant in containers for an extended period. A small retail nursery seldom becomes involved in the latter method. Growing plants in containers for extended periods is usually done by larger or more specialized wholesale nurseries.

The typical nursery operation most readers of this book would be advised to start is a short term container nursery. This means that you would buy bareroot deciduous (trees and shrubs that lose their leaves in fall) stock in a dormant condition and pot it to a selling container anywhere from one to six months before sale. The plants are allowed to root in and produce leaves before they are sold to retail consumers. There is a good deal of variation in how far ahead different

A bare root dormant rose plant trimmed and labeled properly before being containerized.

nursery people pot their dormant plants up but it is obvious that the longer plants are in the pot (within reason) the more established and better quality they are. Evergreens are not too often potted completely bareroot but many short term container growers will use evergreens with a minimum sized soil ball for this purpose. Using a plant with a small soil ball is less expensive than potting with a much larger soil ball and almost as good quality can be delivered to the customer if

A bare root dormant rose plant shortly after being potted in a biodegradable woodfiber container.

plants are allowed to become established in the container long enough.

Various states have laws which regulate the types of pots which may used for short term container nursery stock and laws may also specify the amount of time plants must be in the pots before sale. When getting started in this type of operation you should visit with the local county extension agent or the appropriate division in the state department of

The beautiful result of expert care only nine weeks after potting. Rose plants like this sell in volume at top prices.

agriculture in order to be aware of any regulations which apply.

Local climatic conditions will dictate the exact methods you use to establish container nursery stock. In many of the more humid and moderate climatic regions little initial or subsequent care is required because extremely hard freezes and violent dry wind storms are not common during late

Apple trees which have recently been containerized from dormant bareroot stock. No protection is usually given to trees and shrubs potted in this manner if plants are sufficiently dormant when planted.

winter or early spring when most operators pot up their plants. Wet snows and good rainfall at this time also limit the amount of additional irrigation needed. In harsh climates, like the Rocky Mountains or Desert Southwest, it may be necessary to provide a good deal of care after potting to insure survival.

Evergreens dug with a soil ball and then containerized for sale in woodfiber pots. These plants are easier to care for on the sales lot and easier to move to the customer's location than if left strictly in ball and burlap.

NURSERY STOCK MARKETING

In most sections of the United States, nursery plant sales take place predominantly in the spring months. With the introduction of high quality and readily available containerized stock, there has been a trend towards more summer and fall planting. But consumers are still not especially enthusiastic towards planting at these times. Landscapers are a different story. They simply cannot install all their plants in one or two spring months so they are generally active from the time the frost leaves the ground until it freezes solid in the late fall. Part of the explosion in landscaping business is due to the ready availability of healthy container plants. Planting and marketing of trees and shrubs may continue year round in some southern regions.

Nurseries may be strictly wholesale in their marketing approach, or strictly retail, or a combination of both. The most logical strategy for beginners is to aim their product towards the retail customer. In the early stages of business it is difficult to grow enough plants to realize a satisfactory income if they are sold at wholesale prices. The lowest mark up at which a retail nursery can expect to show a reasonable profit is double the wholesale price; and this is only if you offer plants cash and carry, with no guarantee or special services.

Since most customers will expect plants to be guaranteed through the present growing season and will need rudimentary planting instructions, I suggest a retail price of two and a half to three times the wholesale price. Any further services offered to individual customers must be tacked on to this basic mark up. If you offer any type of installation or landscape service, this should be treated as an entirely different proposition from selling plants. Each service job must be priced individually by the amount of materials and time it will require. And all plants going into a landscape job must be priced at retail.

Some inexperienced nursery owners may be over anxious to make a big sale when a customer wants to buy a lot of plants or have a substantial landscape job done. You cannot give discounts for the larger sale because almost every one of the big purchasers will take full advantage of your guarantee. A large proportion of small customers will never bother to redeem plant guarantees even if they have a perfectly legitimate claim. In my experience, people who purchase a large amount of nursery stock are more likely to give you future headaches than are anonymous crowds whose purchases remain under $50.00.

Anyone who enters the nursery plant business should be fully prepared to give plenty of information about culture and planting and to cheerfully refund guarantees as they are presented, even if the customer's claim is somewhat questionable. A miserly and grudgingly honored guarantee is worse than none at all. Arguments about guarantees are the fastest way to lose customers (and every other potential customer who is bound to hear their sad story).

If you lack a suitable location for retail sales or you do not care to deal with individual customers, starting a profitable wholesale nursery may prove to be your piece of cake. It is more difficult but certainly not impossible. You must find a satisfactory niche which the larger wholesale nurseries are not servicing adequately or which they do not care to service. This usually means producing trees and shrubs which are somewhat rarer in the general marketplace or which require a good deal of individual hand labor.

Landscapers are often a good market for the wholesaler to pursue. A landscaper usually works under project completion deadlines and will gladly pay near retail prices for some special plants which are unobtainable elsewhere.

Whatever marketing strategy you pursue, it is essential to establish a consistent approach early and gear all production work towards a profitable fulfillment of these goals.

Growing plants without an established plan for marketing them profitably is a sure route to failure. A good deal of advance planning is essential to arrive at a realistic and attainable marketing program.

EXAMPLE OF NURSERY
EXPENSES AND PROFITS

I will now show you some simple economic features about the type of small retail nursery you are likely to begin. This representation is simplified a good deal so that the main points are clearly observable.

In order to view our economic model in perspective you must keep the qualifying points listed in Table 5 firmly in mind as you study Tables 6 and 7. One important point which must be stressed is that I have not projected any initial monetary outlay for facilities or equipment. I do this because I assume you already have a small plot of ground available or one which you can rent. The same is true for the transportation needed to complete landscaping jobs projected in the model.

Any incidental equipment needed for start up is included as a part of miscellaneous expenses. In order to be successful with very little risk you must be willing to start with only the bare essentials and work your way up. A new truck and comfortable office might be nice later on but at the start you must make do with existing resources.

The size of nursery projected in this example is not likely to provide a livable family income but merely represents what might be possible during the first year. The operation would need to be expanded a multiple of 2 or 3 times in order to support an average family in moderate style.

The costs represented in Table 6 could be lowered significantly by using recycled pots and by shopping around for less expensive tree and shrub starters or by growing some yourself. Prices paid could sometimes be less than one half of those quoted if you took advantage of special promotions offered by suppliers.

Table 5

Qualifying statements which apply to Tables 6 and 7 of the nursery economic model which follows.

A. Owner will devote 1000 hours per year (equals approximately one half of a normal 40 hour work week) to nursery operation and landscape projects.

B. Cost of care and culture for nursery crops is based upon approximate climatic conditions prevailing in the midwestern United States.

C. Owner is physically capable of doing moderately heavy nursery and landscape work.

D. State laws allow nurseries to containerize plants up to 30 days before sale in approved containers.

E. At least 10000 square feet of reasonably level land can be rented for nursery operations from the owner or others.

F. Water supply is available to nursery.

G. Model assumes 1 complete crop of 1000 containerized 5 gallon trees and 1000 containerized 2 gallon shrubs. With 3% dumpage rate the crop would be reduced to 970 containers of each size.

H. Containers and plant material prices are taken from catalogs of reputable suppliers. They represent neither the lowest or highest prices.

I. All plants to be potted are purchased in dormant state from specialist wholesale growers.

J. Assume plants will be sold retail at the growing location or through use on landscaping projects contracted by the nursery owner.

K. Retail price of $30.00 for 5 gallon containerized trees and $15.00 for containerized shrubs represents the actual price received by the author's retail department in 1992. Guarantee of 6 months given with purchase. Chain store prices are usually cheaper while some independent nurseries may charge more.

L. All plants are sold during the growing season immediately following containerization.

Table 6

Expenses involved in operating a small outdoor tree and shrub container nursery during the growing season. Limited landscape services offered. See text about ways to save on costs.

Variable costs per plant unit produced

Container for 2 gallon shrubs	$0.35
Soil for 2 gallon shrubs	0.30
Container for 5 gallon trees	0.78
Soil for 5 gallon trees	0.60
Dormant bare root shrub for 2 gallon	2.60
Dormant bare root tree for 5 gallon	6.50
Total variable cost per 2 gallon shrub	3.25
Total variable cost per 5 gallon tree	7.88

Fixed operational costs per year for nursery

Land rental for 10000 square feet, 6 months	$600.00
Fertilizer	250.00
Water	400.00
Pest and weed control	200.00
Liability insurance	400.00
Frost protection insulation fabric	200.00
Vehicle usage for 3000 miles at $0.25 per mile	750.00
Miscellaneous tools	250.00
Miscellaneous expenses	500.00
Total fixed operating costs	3550.00

Table 7

Revenues, costs, and profits for operating a small outdoor nursery and landscape service during the growing season only. Refer to Table 5 for qualifying statements.

Calculation of yearly revenues	
Nursery produces 1000 2 gallon shrubs per year at a retail selling price of $15.00 each (1000 x $15.00) .	$15000.00
Nursery produces 1000 5 gallon trees per year at a retail selling price of $30.00 each (1000 x $30.00) .	30000.00
Landscape contract work 300 hours at $25.00 per hour (300 x $25.00)	7500.00
Total gross revenues per year	52500.00

Calculation of yearly selling and production costs	
Cost of advertising to promote business, assume 5% of gross revenues (0.05 x $52500.00)	$2625.00
Extra landscaping and sales help during busiest 8 weeks of season at $6.00 per hour	1920.00
Deduct 3% crop spoilage (0.03 x $45000.00)	1350.00
Fixed operating costs from Table 6	3550.00
Variable cost of planting 1000 2 gallon shrubs (1000 x $3.25)	3250.00
Variable cost of planting 1000 5 gallon trees (1000 x $7.88)	7880.00
Guarantees redeemed for dead trees and shrubs at 5% of net plant sales (0.05 x $43650.00)	2182.50
Total costs per year for selling and production	$22757.50

Calculation of before tax profits	
Total revenues less total selling and production costs ($52500.00 - $22757.50)	$29742.50

The capital requirements necessary to start growing and selling nursery stock are not large if you begin very simply. I have included some landscaping work in the economic model presented in Tables 6 and 7 primarily because it allows you to generate cash flow without significant capital investment. If you perform some landscaping work, fewer trees and shrubs need to be grown to produce the same income. This increases the chances of selling them all at good prices. Marketing plants profitably will be a big challenge in the early years and you must be cautious not to produce more than can be sold. Inventory carry over is a major problem at some nurseries because they constantly produce more plants than they have developed a market for. A high carry over rate causes you to spend a good deal of time caring for the previous year's plant inventory rather than growing new crops.

Doing some landscaping the first year will also let you know if growing plants or installing them in the landscape is more to your liking. You will get a good idea whether landscaping or growing will prove to be the most profitable in your area.

You could sell plants wholesale by offering them to local garden centers, landscapers, or chain stores. But you must remember that the selling price would be at least cut in half and it is not always easy to break into the wholesale market quickly. Most of these businesses order stock at least 6 months in advance and they like to deal with established growers who they feel can deliver the merchandise reliably.

A retail operation with perhaps some landscaping services offered is the only way you can earn a significant income the first few years without investing a good deal of capital. The $29742.50 projected earnings in Tables 6 and 7 for half time work would be decreased greatly if you sold plants for only half as much at wholesale prices. There is opportunity in wholesale nursery production but it takes money and time to become established.

The income you might realize from growing nursery stock can be greatly increased by also selling other related

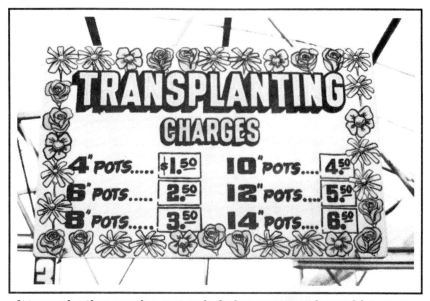

A transplanting service not only helps customer's avoid a messy chore but adds income to the nursery and assures the job is done right. Charges in photograph do not include the price of new pots.

items. Seeds, fertilizers, garden implements, and plant care products are a few of the accessories which might be offered along with trees and shrubs. Your high quality plants will serve as the drawing card to attract customers for other services and merchandise.

I expect a favorable long term trend for tree and shrub sales. You only need to observe the major publicity trees have received on Earth Day in the last few years to realize that the general public is becoming more aware of the ecological significance plants have for the world environment. While many industries spend billions of dollars to promote their product, the nursery trade is receiving billions worth of free advertising!

Potting soil formulated and mixed at the nursery or greenhouse can be a big money maker. One of the highest profit items if it is properly presented and efficiently manufactured.

THE MODERN NURSERY

I have not emphasized the technological side of nursery production in my discussion because most beginners in the industry will have neither the money or technical background to employ the latest methods until they have had a year or two of experience. And the technical aspects of production are of greater importance as one becomes more and more oriented towards wholesale production.

Modern nursery production methods, especially in the early stages of plant growth, may closely parallel the techniques used for greenhouse ornamental production. More and more culture of young nursery stock is taking place in the greenhouse as growers find that the extra cost of indoor facilities is more than made up by the closer control which can be exercised over the crop. In fact, a modern nursery grower may find that training in greenhouse operation and cultural methods is more important to success of a nursery than is a good background in methods used outdoors. Of course, each production phase in a plant's life is important but the trend is clearly towards more intensive indoor culture during the juvenile stage.

The modern nursery, as it becomes larger, is also heavily dependent upon the proper use of machinery and pest and weed control methods. A large nursery can become almost impossible to run unless many of the essential tasks are mechanized. It is no longer possible to find laborers who will work in the fields all day even if they are paid a handsome wage. This is another reason why many growers are moving a good deal of their plant production indoors.

Fortunately, by purchasing young plants from specialists, it is possible for an individual to get started in business without all the newest cultural facilities and machinery. Besides it will take a few years for you to learn what types of modern techniques and facilities you will want to incorporate into your operation as it grows. You should not spend a lot of money on this type of nursery improvement until it can be done wisely.

Chapter 6

PRODUCTION AND MARKETING OF ORNAMENTAL PERENNIAL PLANTS

Perennial plants will be discussed separately from the greenhouse and nursery topics in this book because perennials are becoming more important as a horticultural crop and because their production and marketing is sufficiently different to warrant some special comments. Many businesses which we would normally call nurseries are, in fact, specialist producers of perennial plants. And some greenhouse owners are now concentrating their efforts upon perennials.

There is no question that ornamental perennials are now receiving more public attention than in the past. Although perennials may have been proportionately even more important in the landscape before the current boom in annual flower usage arrived, they were primarily a private preoccupation. Gardeners would locate particular varieties they wanted and then trade seed and plant divisions amongst themselves. Perhaps the reason perennials are now becoming more commercialized is that a fast paced lifestyle does not lend itself to leisurely treasure hunts and subsequent bargaining sessions for the desired varieties. And many new gardeners have the impression that if they plant perennials, they will save time in the future since the plants will come back every year and require very little care.

PERENNIAL BUSINESS EASY AND ECONOMICAL TO START

If you are looking for a horticultural business which you can start with very little money and operate part time in your own backyard—this is it! A very high return on the money and time you invest is possible. Although there are several large growers on the national scene and although perennials are often featured as mail order offers, there is generally a shortage of locally grown fresh perennials in almost every section of the country.

Of course the amount of money and time you invest in a perennial plant venture will be a determining factor in how large and prosperous your business ultimately becomes, but it is easy to start in this speciality on a very small scale and gradually expand as your resources and interest grow. Other horticultural enterprises also offer this opportunity but perhaps not to the same degree.

Although the local gardening market for perennials is not likely to be as large as for annual flowers or nursery stock, it is generally less competitive. If the proper production and marketing methods are employed, it is possible to realize a greater percentage return for perennials than it is for the more common plant items carried in garden centers, plant stores, and mass outlets. For a small perennial grower, even the wholesale market may be a suitable entry point because a relatively high unit price is possible and there are often no other local wholesale growers.

Because the total market for perennials is fairly small most larger greenhouses and nurseries are reluctant to begin specific cultural and distribution programs involving them. The big operators want to move mountains of merchandise through standardized production schemes. They are not interested in limited demand items. This is the perfect situation for small growers to supply the local market at highly profitable prices.

The costs involved in establishing a perennial plant business will vary greatly with the specific methods employed but it is possible to get started with almost no initial outlay and with very little operating expenses. This is truly a business which you can begin in your own backyard.

Perennials command premium prices in most localities. Even on sale there is plenty of room for profit on these medium sized plants. Photographed in 1991.

DIFFERENT METHODS
OF PERENNIAL CULTURE

Perennials have undergone much the same changes in culture from bare root to containerization as have trees and shrubs. A small but growing proportion are now also being sold as juvenile seedlings straight from the greenhouse. I believe the main reason why perennials have not developed into a large segment of the horticultural industry as yet is because growers have been unable to develop an economical method of containerization which allows reasonably priced plants to be sold in flower over a long period of time.

Containerization at an economical price can surely be achieved easily, I have done it myself. But, except for isolated varieties, I'm not certain that perennials will ever be routinely brought into flower in these inexpensive containers. Much depends upon what one considers inexpensive. My definition is that the price of flowering perennials should be fairly close to that of a bedding plant pack of flowering petunias or impatiens.

Why must the perennials be in flower if a truly large volume of plants are to be sold? Because the average consumer will not as yet purchase non-flowering garden plants in any great numbers. This is just a fact of life! People buy flowers because they are pretty and if a person can't see the beauty at the time of purchase, it is left to the poor substitutes of pictures and imagination to convey the message.

You however, need not speculate about the future market for ornamental perennials. The present market size and price structure are favorable enough to make good money now.

For those of you who may not be familiar with the life cycle of perennials, I will provide a short outline and then show some of the ways perennials might be prepared for market. Perennials are reproduced by any number of means, depending upon the variety. Cuttings, root divisions, and seed propagation are the most common methods. Plants propagated in one growing season normally need to be subjected to a cooler winter rest period before they will bloom.

You can market the plants in small containers as actively growing juveniles shortly after propagation, in which case they will not generally bloom in the garden that season. Juvenile plants may also be stepped up to larger containers or planted to the field, in either case being subjected to cooler

A "flat" of excellent perennial Coreopsis seedlings ready for sale with color picture tags or for transplanting to larger containers. You may produce seedlings on site or purchase them from specialist growers.

conditions through the winter so that flowering occurs the following growth season. Perennials which have been cold treated in the field can be sold as dormant plants naked of soil or established in containers after digging. Plants which were containerized the previous year as juveniles are simply allowed to begin growth or they may be stepped up again to larger containers before active growth starts in earnest.

Color picture tags are essential if you sell perennials. Not only do they give cultural information, they also allow customers to know exactly what the flowers will look like.

Offering perennials in the juvenile stage with color picture tags attached results in a quick turnover of inventory and a modest price to consumers. Dormant bare root plants can be sold fairly inexpensively but they allow only a very short timespan for marketing. Planting cold treated bare root perennials to large containers or allowing cold treatment to take place after plants are established in the larger containers results in perhaps the highest quality plants for consumer use but also the most expensive.

You will have to decide what the best method of handling perennials is for your particular situation. Bare root marketing is declining in acceptability to most gardeners so I would encourage you to think very hard before choosing this alternative.

THE ECONOMICS OF GROWING AND SELLING PERENNIALS

A small plot of land which you own or rent can produce a tremendous number of perennial plants if it is intensively managed. A square of your backyard measuring only 40 feet to a side can hold 3600 perennials potted in 1 gallon containers.

If you sold these plants wholesale at $3.00 apiece you would have an income of about $10000.00 before a few modest expenses were deducted. Granted, this isn't enough income to make you feel rich but it is very good money if you spend only a few hours weekly working at it and you have very little money invested. All you have to do is put in the same effort required by a large recreational garden plot. Table 8 outlines the economics of this type of enterprise if we assume no rental is paid for the small piece of ground needed. The presentation is simple because the operation is simple.

A group of one gallon perennials on sale in early season before significant bloom. This is the size of container specified in the accompanying tables.

Table 8

Expenses and profits of a small backyard perennial plant growing operation. Expenses can be lowered greatly by using recycled pots and starting plants from seed or cuttings rather than buying both items.

Purchase 3600 small plants from a propagator specialist at $0.30 each (3600 x $0.30)	$1080.00
Purchase 3600 gallon pots new at $0.20 each (3600 x $0.20)	720.00
Expenses of miscellaneous items: extra water, fertilizer, tools, pest control, insulation blankets for winter protection	600.00
Total expenses	2400.00
Total revenues from selling 3420 gallon perennials wholesale at $3.00 each. 180 plants or 5% of crop assumed wasted or lost. (3420 x $3.00)	10260.00
Total profits ($10260.00 - $2400.00)	7860.00

Perennial plants are perhaps my first choice recommendation for those individuals who have a limited budget to begin a horticultural business. This type of enterprise can be started by almost anyone, anywhere. I favor marketing perennials primarily on the wholesale level for two main reasons. First, it simplifies the situation; you do not need to have a location suitable for retail activity and you do not need to staff it all the time. Secondly, since perennials are not generally a big volume seller; competition from larger growers is not usually severe. This situation allows you to make an adequate profit even when selling at wholesale. Most garden centers and mass outlets will welcome the opportunity to buy high quality local perennials because they have a hard time finding them. If growing ornamental perennials is something you want to investigate further, the suggested literature section at the back of this book contains a booklet which explores this topic further.

NUMEROUS PERENNIAL VARIETIES REQUIRE PROMOTION

As I mentioned previously, the perennial plant market is not exceptionally large at this moment. The gardening benefits provided by thousands of perennial varieties are not easily conveyed to the mass of consumers. A big pot of annual petunias in full bloom is its own best advertisement. Perennials are not generally of this gaudy, self proclaiming nature; often they bloom only briefly and then perhaps only in a delicate manner. It takes an educational effort on the part of perennial growers and sellers to introduce the casual gardener to the many and varied benefits perennials can offer.

The color picture tag is perhaps the biggest help in selling perennials. It lets the consumer have some idea of what the plant looks like in bloom and can convey essential cultural information. Tags allow you to sell plants out of bloom and thus greatly extend the marketing season.

It is hard to imagine the extent of perennial plant diversity. There are literally thousands of varieties. This situation provides both advantage and disadvantage for growers. Advantage in that it allows for continuous introduction of new cultivars to the market but disadvantage in that consumers must be educated in the use and benefits of each introduction. The perennial grower must be willing to make this educational commitment in order to assure success. Much of your work in marketing perennials must be aimed at promoting products in an effective and economical manner. In perennials the old saying "the more you tell, the more you sell" is especially true.

Chapter 7

THE RETAIL HORTICULTURAL BUSINESS

Most of you probably began reading this book because you were interested in growing plants for profit, not particularly in selling plants for profit. Plant enthusiasts, like myself, just naturally gravitate toward the growing end of horticulture. They don't generally get excited a great deal by the marketing aspects of business. But if you want to make a living by growing plants you must learn how to sell them profitably. There is no getting around this fact.

A few people actually like to sell plants more than they like to grow them and some people are not in the proper situation to be growers. I offer the following brief discussion to those of you who find yourself in this category. I will deal with horticultural businesses whose primary activity is selling plants rather than growing them.

Even though growing is my chief interest, I must admit that selling plants is usually the more profitable aspect of horticultural business. Neither growing or selling is more important but if we separate the two sides of the equation for close inspection, the act of selling is generally the more crucial factor which determines profitability.

I do not pretend to understand why this is so, it certainly seems to be true in other commercial pursuits as well. My purpose in dwelling upon this fact is not to discourage you from a career growing plants but to impress upon you the importance marketing will have upon your business and also to introduce the idea that perhaps your personal situation may be more amenable to a strictly retail horticultural business which requires no production labor or facilities.

A vertically integrated horticultural business (one which both produces and sells the plant merchandise) is more often extremely successful than is one which is concentrated specifically upon growing or selling. But there are some very sound reasons for beginning your horticultural career as a retailer only. For the sake of brevity I will list these reasons in Table 9 and omit further comment unless it is essential.

One of the drawbacks of retail business is that there is more competition in this area. Many of the reasons for being a retailer or grower are a double edged sword. Seldom is a factor totally advantageous or deleterious. Business activity involves a process of choosing the most appropriate path to accomplish objectives. You must carefully weigh each alternative and select the one which you will lead most certainly to success.

Each of the business opportunities discussed in this book could be entered from a strictly retail approach. I hope you will keep this in mind as you begin to evaluate the different options available.

Although I do not want to present a detailed discussion of how to run a retail business, I would like to mention one extremely important point. It concerns business location. If you have no production facilities or any other special attraction which will encourage customers to visit your place of business, it is obvious that a retail store lives or dies primarily upon how well situated the retail location is to bring merchandise and customers together. How much business you do will greatly depend upon the number of people who are exposed to your plants and related products. One of the primary ways of obtaining this exposure is by selecting a high traffic location. An anonymous commentator once remarked that there are 3 key ingredients to success in retail business "location, location, location."

Table 9

Primary reasons for beginning a horticultural business with special or sole emphasis upon the retail aspects. Statements are generalized and will not be true in every case.

A. Retail requires less initial capital.

B. Allows you to learn about the business before committing capital and time to a growing operation.

C. You will develop a "feel" for the market possibilities before you implement growing programs to satisfy the market.

D. Smaller businesses can produce more sales volume per dollar invested by concentrating upon retail aspects.

E. The lead time required for entering a retail business is less than that necessary to begin growing crops.

F. With less money, effort, facilities, and inventory committed to a retail business, it is easier to abandon if it proves unsuccessful.

G. Allows you to place emphasis on one aspect of the business before engaging in another.

H. If your local market requires many diverse plant products, it may be easier to buy than to learn how to grow a diversity of crops.

I. A surplus of growers with a general lack of retailers in your area would make the retail business aspect look better relative to growing.

J. Retail allows you to concentrate time on offering a broad line of plant merchandise without having to learn the details about every variety.

K. While retailing requires a good deal of business knowledge, it does not require extensive technical knowledge about different varieties.

L. Retailing does not place a large inventory at risk to natural hazards when compared to a growing operation.

Many independent operators are able to obtain super retail locations by leasing space next to supermarkets, discount stores, and hardware stores.

Chapter 8

ADDITIONAL HORTICULTURAL SPECIALITY BUSINESSES

There are many ways to make money by growing or selling plants or providing plant services. I have covered a few of the more likely and widely available opportunities in some detail. Perhaps you have not found a speciality among these which strikes your fancy or maybe none of them seems possible under the personal circumstances in which you find yourself. A brief listing of additional horticultural enterprises might help you find a more suitable choice to match up with your talents and resources.

I have chosen not to discuss these miscellaneous horticultural businesses at length for a variety of purposes. Mostly because it is a practical necessity to limit discussion of certain topics in order that the overall purpose of this book is not lost by excessive detail. But you should not interpret my decision to abbreviate as an indication that any of these businesses are less worthy of consideration than the ones I treated more completely. Any one of the following possibilities could be exactly what you are looking for and each could be highly profitable under the proper circumstances.

The secret to financial success in horticultural speciality businesses will not be found in some universally applicable rule or equation but rather in finding the particular economic opportunity which allows you to take advantage of market forces special to your local surroundings. If these unique market forces can be matched with your natural talents, the combination can result in an amazingly successful business. There is no effortless way to find this happy combination, it takes a good deal of investigation regarding available opportunities and some realistic soul searching to determine just what your special talents are. Hopefully I will be able to start you on this process by pointing out some of the benefits and drawbacks to be found in particular situations. .

In general, the following business opportunities are of a rather specialized nature and their applicability may be limited to a narrow range of circumstances. Often the people who are already active in these specialized fields tend towards an exaggerated view of how important and potentially rewarding their speciality is. I cannot fault them greatly for this since it is likely I engage in some of the same behavior in regards to my areas of interest. But we must be aware of the situation and try to be as realistic as possible.

My caution to you is that as you read information about a specific field of interest or discuss it with promoters or activists, make sure all the facts presented seem to add up properly and that the overall proposition appears to make sense. While it cannot be denied that there are many legitimate business opportunities in every one of these fields, it is also true that a certain amount of self-serving exaggeration may sometimes overshadow the hard headed economic facts when enthusiasts present their case to you.

In most of these horticultural speciality businesses, particularly if you start small, there is no need for high priced consultants nor should you pay more than absolutely necessary for essential equipment. Carefully investigate any offers you receive to make sure they are legitimate and cost effective. I have seen more than one enterprise in horticulture where the only person to make money is the expert consultant or the individual who sells supposedly required equipment.

GREENHOUSE VEGETABLE PRODUCTION

Perhaps no other area of horticulture strikes the imagination as strongly as does growing vegetables, especially tomatoes, indoors. And with good reason; there is an almost unlimited demand for this crop. If vegetables could be produced in the greenhouse at prices which were truly competitive with the open air farmer's price, we would witness the largest construction boom in greenhouses which has ever occurred.

Greenhouse grown vegetables can be sold only because they are of higher quality than field grown produce or because they are available when field crops are out of season. Crops grown indoors can seldom compete pricewise with those grown outdoors. This is the central fact behind why there is not more indoor production of food crops. When food crops are grown under cover, the very competitive and commodity like nature of vegetable prices tends to make profitable operation of these greenhouses extremely difficult.

Throughout this book I have stressed that the lucrative nature of horticultural speciality crops is enhanced by their non commodity like market position. In other words, these speciality crops are relatively small so that institutionalized markets do not exist for them. Prices are struck between the individual producers and buyers, not established by an impersonal market force. This is the type of situation which favors smaller, innovative growers. Of course everyone must realize that these markets we speak of differ only in degree. Individual farmers in the giant wheat market may occasionally be able to realize some competitive price advantage due to their shrewdness and a greenhouse grower of petunias is often constrained somewhat by price structures prevailing in the informal petunia market. But, generally, the larger the market size, the more competitive pricing and production becomes.

Anyone who wants to begin a commercial greenhouse vegetable growing operation must evaluate the advantages and drawbacks of this business carefully. Demand for the product is immense but prices are normally fairly low. Production costs can easily outrun the wholesale prices received for crops unless they are grown efficiently. And there is not much chance of selling any significant part of your crops at higher retail prices because the established market channel for vegetables is in the supermarket.

Most successful vegetable greenhouses are fairly large and they are generally located in population centers where quality produce of one variety or another is in short supply at different times of the year. The newer facilities being constructed today are mostly highly automated and capital intensive. Some very large corporations have become active in this horticultural speciality, not always successfully.

Depending upon the tax codes applying at the time, there may be financial incentives other than simple buy and sell factors to consider when setting up a vegetable greenhouse. Some of these operations have shown tax shelter opportunities in the past. In certain locations there is a tendency for local government agencies and economic development groups to help finance businesses which involve greenhouse vegetable growing. You may be lucky enough to find very favorable financing and business incentives offered in your area.

Ordinary people usually envision a vegetable greenhouse as one in which tomatoes are grown hydroponically (in nutrient solution without soil). But, in fact, leaf lettuce and cucumbers are probably the leading crops at present. And there are many greenhouses which use some form of soil-like mixture as a growth medium rather than growing in gravel or water troughs. The nutrient supply may be basically similar to that used in pure hydroponic systems but several methods for delivering this solution to the roots are presently employed.

One big advantage to greenhouse vegetable growing is that many equipment and material suppliers offer more or less cook book instructional services. Since a grower is often engaged in production of a single variety, these standardized methods may be quite effective. Be advised, however, that there are many alternative methods. Do not rely blindly upon advice from someone else instead of using your own good judgment. Some companies even claim to offer effective marketing services for growers who do not wish to be bothered with this phase of the business.

Since growing greenhouse vegetables is a popular subject, there are several excellent technical books to help the newcomer along.

If you are interested in this field you should first check out the economics of marketing and growing in your area very carefully and realistically. Do not be overenthusiastic simply because the project seems glamorous. Evaluate equipment and material suppliers extensively for reliability and price. References from established growers should be checked out carefully before you make any substantial investment commitments. My personal opinion of the opportunities in this horticultural speciality is that it is not one of the easier businesses to enter on a limited budget. And if you become involved, it should be with the idea of eventually expanding to a large enough size to compete efficiently. The existence of a large market and standardized growing methods are potential benefits under some circumstances.

HERB PRODUCTION AND MARKETING

The separation of herb and vegetable production into different topics is purely arbitrary. Except for some differences in the market structure, most of my comments about greenhouse vegetables could be applied equally well to herbs.

Although herbs have been grown commercially since time immemorial, it has only been in the last few years that much thought has been given them in the United States as a separate entity apart from other agricultural crops. Fresh herbs from the greenhouse have especially received attention recently. Whether or not this notoriety will become permanently established remains to be seen. Fresh herb production indoors is concentrated in the more cosmopolitan population centers where demand is being spearheaded by use in exclusive restaurants. Supermarkets are beginning to pick up on the trend toward fresh herb use and routinely offer some of the more common varieties in their produce selection.

If the current preoccupation with gourmet dining among our population continues, it is possible that both indoor and outdoor culture of specialized herbs will skyrocket.

In some ways the herb market resembles that for flowers and ornamental plants. It is still rather small (as it is for ornamentals) when compared to more basic agricultural crops; and there is a wide assortment of varieties which are meant to be used under particular circumstances in food preparation, semi-medicinal treatments, scents, and other assorted purposes. This market structure lends itself to generally higher prices and offers opportunity for smaller producers to find a specialized niche which is highly profitable. One characteristic which the herb market does not share with ornamentals at present is the existence of widespread independent retail opportunity. While flower shops, nurseries, and garden centers flourish in almost every small town in America, shops specializing only in herbs have not yet been able to become successful on so general a basis. Only where their popularity is greater and where sufficient population is present are special retail herb shops able to prosper.

Thus, although the wholesale price paid for herbs may be rather attractive in most locations, selling your herb produce at retail prices is not a viable option except in those areas where circumstances combine to allow enough volume for establishment of independent retail shops. The market for herbs seems to be increasing but this phenomenon is not of sufficient duration as yet to confirm that herbs will become a major and stable horticultural speciality crop.

If you chose to enter this field I suggest you be aware that demand for herbs could decrease rapidly if their appeal in gourmet cooking and semi-medicinal purposes wanes to any extent. Ornamental foliage plants suffered a similar fate a few years ago; there was near insatiable demand during the late 70's and early 80's when leading decorators and magazines promoted the use of interior plants but as these opinion leaders moved on to other interests, foliage demand decreased rapidly from the boom levels.

I believe that if a sustained bonanza in herb production and sales is to become reality, it will result from demand related to their increased use in mainstream medical applications. In this situation the prices of raw product are of little concern to consumers; quality factors and steady year round availability become the dominant requirements. If such circumstances developed we could see prices for high quality medicinal herbs reach gold rush levels.

There is now much preliminary activity in medical circles regarding derivation of medicines from plants (there always has been a good deal); but, as yet, not much of this activity has resulted in widespread practical opportunities for plant growers to fill specific needs for crops. This situation could change quickly if a few major drugs were developed which depend upon plant materials requiring a good deal of expertise to produce.

MAIL ORDER HORTICULTURE

The idea of selling plants through the mail probably doesn't occur to a great number of people. After all, why ship plants hundreds or even thousands of miles to customers when you are surrounded by potential buyers in your neighborhood? There are a couple of good reasons: first, you may live in a rural location where customers are far and few between; and secondly, you may wish to specialize in growing a particular variety or group of varieties for which there is insufficient local demand but which has significant potential on the national scene.

Selling by mail order can be one of the most profitable and worry free methods of doing business if certain basic requirements are satisfied. Table 10 lists the most important points necessary for a successful mail order plant business.

There is no need to limit your mail order effort to plants; non-plant horticultural products are even easier to handle and ship by this means.

Table 10

Basic requirements which must be met to successfully sell horticultural products through mail order.

A. Product must possess weight, shape, size, and durability characteristics which allow for economical and safe shipping.

B. Plant products must be of such a nature as to reach customer in good shape even when subjected to the normal rigors of shipping process (heat, cold, rough handling).

C. Sufficient product line must be available to generate a critical mass of total sales. Or alternatively, a single product offer must be popular enough to generate profitable volume.

D. A customer list must be developed for use in selling additional products.

E. Products must conform to requirements of shipping companies and to state, national, and local laws.

F. Product must possess characteristics which allow it to be advertised effectively and economically.

G. Product must actually satisfy customer so future orders will be made by that customer.

H. The mail order offer package must be designed to yield a profitable combination. Components of the offer are product, price, advertisability, audience, volume, and all the various aspects which integrate with one another to form the total offer.

I. An advertisement must be constructed which presents the offer in terms that pull enough orders to be profitable.

J. All sales must be carefully recorded and evaluated to determine the effectiveness of different aspects of the total mail order offer. Example: orders resulting from advertisements in different magazines must be tabulated to determine which magazines were profitable and which were not.

Probably the biggest mistake prospective mail order entrepreneurs make is to expect that a single hot merchandise item will make their business successful. Mail order is like any other business, profits are usually built up over a period of time as a customer base is accumulated. New products are then added and sold to these existing customers.

Mail order can be a rewarding method of making money but success does not magically appear. A person seldom becomes rich in mail order by getting a flash idea, running a few advertisements, and then simply waiting for cash to arrive in the mail box.

Don't give up if you fail to make money on the first try. Sometimes it takes several experimental attempts before the right elements of a mail order offer are brought together into a profitable combination. But when this is accomplished, it can mean a lasting source of relatively trouble free income.

People like to purchase by mail order if they can feel safe about sending their money to you. An ironclad guarantee of satisfaction is the best way to convince customers to part with their money. If your offer is legitimate, an unconditional guarantee will result in a very low percent of returns.

Mail order is convenient for everyone concerned. You do not have to leave your place of business and the consumer receives the merchandise at their front door. What could be easier? This is why companies often receive a higher price for merchandise through mail order than if it was sold in a conventional store. Mail order saves the customer time and travel expenses.

INTERIOR AND EXTERIOR LANDSCAPING

Many individuals and firms providing interior and exterior landscaping services do not actually grow any significant proportion of the plant material which is used in their work. Being both a grower and landscaper allows you to develop an increased expertise about plants and provides access to a ready inventory of plant material for installation jobs. But operating in two specialities requires more time and capital.

In its simplest aspects, a landscaping business may be started with almost no capital or previous experience. This is why there are so many small operators to provide competition in this field. In order to stand out from the crowd you must develop an expertise which customers will immediately recognize. If you don't they will do the job themselves or hire the neighborhood handy man.

When deciding how much you should charge for your services, it is essential that careful account be taken of exactly what you have to offer. Your fee should include a basic charge for the actual work to be done and a premium on top of this for the knowledge and expertise you contribute.

True landscaping is a combination of technical and artistic work. Hopefully, you can offer both services in the ideal mix. But if you aren't an artist, don't worry, most jobs require only that you be able to organize and carry out a technically correct plant installation project.

Landscaping pays the best when you specialize in commercial or public projects and buildings. Small jobs for the individual homeowner are less complicated but generally offer less opportunity for profit. However, the big commercial jobs usually go to firms with an established track record of financial and technical capability. You will have to work your way up to the plum jobs. Most commercial and public landscape projects are awarded on a bid basis and you must be in a position to receive notification when a job is coming up for bid.

Well known firms receive bid notifications from architects, parks directors, or general contractors; new entries to the landscape business will have to seek out opportunities to bid on jobs. Most localities have a bid newsletter or notification service to which landscapers can subscribe. This service allows you to quickly pinpoint potential landscape jobs without running all over town to different job sites; and it allows you to get your bid in early before contracts have already been awarded.

Submitting a bid for landscaping services is no easy job. It is often the most critical ingredient to success. An inflated

Local businesses and government entities are important sources of landscaping income. Many jobs do not require project design, they entail only proper installation of vegetation.

bid proposal might lose you the job while too low a bid will result in a financial loss on the project. Costs must be estimated realistically for all aspects of the job which you are expected to complete. Do not leave any detail up to question.

Unexpected difficulties at the job site are one of the most common reasons why contractors lose money on landscaping projects. Look the job over very carefully and try to foresee problems which might arise. When your cost estimate is complete then add about 5% to compensate for unpredictable difficulties. Sometimes no unforeseen problems will be encountered but in other cases their cost will exceed 5% of the job total.

You will not get far in the landscaping business unless a realistic guarantee is offered and honored. In the long run it is better to ask a few dollars more for services in order to provide liberal guarantees which do not place an undue burden of proof upon the customer.

Most readers of this book are aware that outdoor landscaping is a common service offered in almost every town. But many of you may be surprised at the opportunities available in landscaping building interiors. This is a fast growing industry and offers a good deal of opportunity, especially to those people who would find outdoor jobs too physically demanding. Indoor projects generally do not require as much heavy work nor are you subjected to extreme climatic conditions.

PLANT CARE SERVICES

Given the busy lifestyle of today's families, the plant care field can only grow in volume and variety of work available for the horticultural specialist. The problem with this field, as with landscaping, is that everyone who needs a few extra dollars believes they can turn a profit caring for other people's plants.

In order to avoid the often unprofitable and unrewarding competition with amateurs, you must carefully and deliberately distinguish yourself from the crowd by stressing the knowledgeable, professional, and completely reliable nature of your services. There are many businesses and individuals who will gladly pay extra for the peace of mind your expert plant care brings when compared to that provided by on again, off again amateurs.

Everyone is familiar with the variety of plant care services offered to private consumers for their lawns, trees, and gardens. What you may not realize is the tremendous demand for these and further services which originate in the business and public sector. Most businesses would prefer to have a reliable expert take care of their indoor and outdoor landscaping rather than taking one of their own workers away from his or her normal duties. There are often formal union or informal professional rules which prevent employees from working outside their expertise area. Do you think the Postal Service or Internal Revenue Service dares ask regular employees to fertilize the lawn or shine the leaves on indoor plants?

Although there is currently a good deal more potential work for plant care specialists in the outdoor landscape, the need for care of indoor plants is growing rapidly and there is probably less competition in this aspect. Working with indoor plants has several advantages: it is cleaner and less physically demanding, it is less seasonal in nature, and generally requires less equipment.

Whether you care for plants indoors or out, there are a couple of points you must remember to be successful. Repeat customers will eventually be the backbone of your business; you must be reliable, courteous, and do a good job in order to expect their future business. These valuable characteristics should entitle you to adequate compensation. Ask for reasonable payment in return for the knowledge and diligence you provide. And don't take on jobs which are so small as to make it impossible to turn a profit. Travel time and entering the job site can take up a lot of your day if you accept assignments which offer only a few minutes of actual work. You must charge the customer not only for the time spent on the job but also for the time it takes to schedule the appointment, travel to the job site, present a bill, and take care of bookwork afterward.

You can get into the plant care field, either indoors or outdoors, with very little capital and there is lots of work available if you look for it. But you face a battle convincing customers that your expert services are worth more than the many amateurs willing to work cheaper. A sales program emphasizing the many benefits of expert care must be developed. Simply walking in and asking for the job will not generate much work, especially if your prices are higher.

HORTICULTURAL THERAPY SERVICES

Why are gardening and related horticultural pastimes the most popular leisure activities in the United States? Is it because they offer us a chance to save money on food products or the opportunity to make money by selling useful products to others? While a few horticultural enthusiasts do achieve these practical goals, the great majority indulge in this hobby because it gives satisfaction, a bit of physical exercise, and, above all, a chance to relax and forget the mental pressures which life brings.

Mental health experts and physical therapists have long recognized the benefit which horticultural activities offer the human mind and body.

Horticultural therapy programs are common at many institutions but it is almost impossible to locate such service programs which are available to individuals once they are no longer associated with an institution on a regular basis.

I believe that providing well conceived horticultural programs and products for people to use in continuing, non-institutional therapy is one of the most neglected areas of horticultural business. It is a field which offers the possibility of extremely attractive financial rewards while simultaneously reducing the suffering of human beings. Since this field is not yet truly established, not much can be said about how to proceed in setting up a business which specializes in it.

One thing which is obvious is that the people who enter this type of business should have a background in mental or physical therapy, as well as horticulture. Integration of these two elements composing a therapy program is a necessity.

Any therapy program must be well coordinated with established health and mental care institutions and professionals. No one could hope to be successful in this type of service business unless the program evidenced unquestioned professional expertise and enjoyed a positive relationship with potential referring institutions and professional individuals.

Under existing concepts of insurance coverage and public aid programs, it is likely that horticultural therapy services would have be financed by the individual person receiving benefits unless the therapy service was associated with or prescribed through agencies or individuals recognized by the insurance companies or public aid programs.

As with any new and relatively untested concept, there would be many problems associated with developing a horticultural therapy service. But the reward for pioneering into territory where the fee structure is already high and competition is non-existent could be immense.

MISCELLANEOUS HORTICULTURAL SERVICES AND PRODUCTS

We could continue indefinitely listing and discussing different horticultural specialities which can be engaged in for profit. The projects I have presented appear to be the most likely candidates for business opportunities in which a large number of horticultural enthusiasts could participate easily. They are suitable, with few exceptions, to almost every locality in the United States and Canada.

If none of the specialties I have mentioned appeals to you as a business proposition or if each one offers little likelihood of success under your particular circumstances, don't despair! With a little research and imagination I'm sure you can create an original idea for commercial application which is uniquely suited to your special talents and resources.

Perhaps you live on a farm in a completely rural area and feel there is little you can do to participate in the horticultural success story. But have you ever thought of raising wildflower seed, or Christmas trees, or lawn sod, or perhaps dried herbs and flowers on at least part of your acreage? Each of these horticultural specialities can be done very profitably if you have the wherewithal and farming expertise to participate effectively! Most of my readers do not have access to the amount of land, water, or machinery necessary for these operations; but perhaps they are already part of your present farm operation.

Some localities may possess special advantages which have not as yet been recognized for certain horticultural crops. The advantage may be one of proximity to new markets, availability of raw materials, climate, or other factors. Perhaps your area has abundantly available substrate for mushroom culture or maybe it possesses the climate and water resources which are perfect for growing aquarium plants. Who knows?

The only way you can identify these more unusual opportunities is to make yourself aware of all of the exotic horticultural activities people participate in and then see if any of these appear to fit in with your local conditions. A good way to locate possible opportunities is to go through advertisements, especially the classified, in horticulture related magazines. And don't be discouraged because someone else already does a certain thing; that only means it is potentially profitable.

My own situation is a case in point. Although growing and selling ornamental plants has been very financially rewarding to me, I have almost exhausted the market potential in my sparsely populated region. And besides, I am interested in areas of horticulture other than strictly growing and selling. After a good deal of thought and research the idea came to me that my educational and business background would provide the necessary ingredients for a successful sideline in horticultural writing. I can't say I've gotten rich from writing about horticulture and business but it has provided a significant second income and it is a rewarding endeavor in itself.

This is the type of personal exploration you need to perform in order to identify the opportunities best suited for your circumstances. I'm sure you will find some field of horticulture to work in that offers financial security while also enriching the other aspects of life.

Part III

HOW TO GET STARTED AND SUCCEED IN BUSINESS

People who enjoy learning how to grow plants usually have some favorable character traits which are useful in the business world. Horticulturists must be patient, willing to work hard, and acutely observant of their environment. Each of these attributes is critical to success in business. But horticulturists are notoriously poor practitioners of the various administrative, marketing, financial, and personnel management activities which we normally expect are the special domain of the business person.

While you need not be a Wall Street genius to succeed at some form of horticultural business, you must attend to at least the most elementary management activities necessary to avoid financial chaos. If you cannot force yourself to perform these essential business related details, then perhaps your best option is take on a partner who is willing and able to do so, or make use of a financial planning and accounting service.

Whether you decide to farm out some of the strictly business related activities of your enterprise or do them yourself, only you can determine the more basic strategic concepts which will influence the general success or failure of the business. You are the one who will ultimately suffer if important business decisions and actions are left unattended. In addition to formulating a sound horticultural program, you must make adequate plans for the business related aspects of your entrepreneurial venture. Remember you are running a business; not indulging a hobby!

Part III if this book will give you an outline of how to start a successful business and how to make sure being in business accomplishes your ultimate goal of leading a happy and rewarding life. I will not attempt to provide details about particular subjects unless it seems that they are especially relevant to a discussion of business in horticulture. If you wish to investigate certain business concepts further, your local library contains many books which pertain to small business operation.

Chapter 9

COLLECT INFORMATION AND DEVELOP A PLAN

Now that you have surveyed the general field of speciality horticulture and learned a few details about particular business opportunities, perhaps you have decided to take the plunge and start an exciting new venture. The first task is to develop a concrete and effective course of action which will lead to success. In order to devise a plan you must gather more detailed information about the chosen field of activity. Basically you will want to build a business plan which addresses the specifics relating to marketing, product production or supply sources, and general business practices.

You could approach this task like some major companies and institutions do; by hiring a consultant. But I assume you don't have the kind of money these consultants want for their time and that, more than likely, you could do twice as good a job if you put your mind to it. Lets face it, the practice of hiring consultants arises in large part from the desire of individuals to cover their own backside. If something goes wrong with the project, they can always blame the consultant instead of themselves.

HOW TO FIND INFORMATION

Where can you find the type of information you are looking for? The most obvious and most inexpensive source

I can think of is in quality books. A couple of hours with a run of the mill consultant will most likely cost upwards of $500.00. For this amount you could buy 10 or 20 books about the subject and feel reasonably confident that the authors of these books are some of the most well informed and successful members of the horticultural industry. As a source of the

Books like the one pictured offer the most efficient and economical means of locating information necessary to start and operate a horticultural business. Frequently used volumes should be added to your personal library for handy reference.

basic information you will need to run a business in horticulture, there is simply no economical substitute for books.

Trade magazines are another informational bargain. Although magazines will not give you the type of well organized knowledge you can get out of books, they will include new cultural and variety developments, product news, advertisements from suppliers, and general industry news about trade fairs and seminars. A look at the suggested literature section in the back of this book will give you a good start in locating the most useful books and trade magazines for your business enterprise.

I have already discussed some of the major means of gathering information in chapter 2, Part I of this book. There is no need to emphasize the sources of information any further; but you should realize that after deciding to enter business in a particular field, you will need to gather as much factual information as possible. Concrete business plans require specific data rather than nebulous general impressions.

At this time you need to generate as much numerical data about the marketing and financial aspects of the planned new business as is possible. This process is not easy and seldom can you expect it to yield answers with more than a 10% range of accuracy. But 10% or 20% accuracy is better than relying upon wild guesses. Numerical data forces you to think in exact terms rather than simply day dreaming about generalities.

You may wish to confirm some of the information gathered from different sources by making some private surveys concerning prices, amounts of plants sold by different outlets, and customer preferences. It is no trouble to gather price data; all you need do is visit a number of establishments and write down the prices or obtain a price list.

As concerns volume, a rough estimate of sales made by different outlets can be tabulated by simply observing their operation for sample periods of time while recording each sale by the amount and type of merchandise involved.

Customer preferences may be harder to uncover since most customers you observe will simply be reacting to the merchandise placed before them rather than selecting what they really would like if it were available. Some of this difficulty can be overcome by actually interviewing a number of potential customers to determine what their likes and dislikes are.

BASIC BUSINESS PRACTICES

There are some routine mechanics to observe no matter what type of business is being set up. You should become aware of all the local, state, and federal laws and regulations which apply to business in general. On the local level you can obtain a list of general requirements by visiting the city and county administrative offices. Be particularly careful to obtain a copy of local zoning regulations; and make sure you understand them before making any decisions about locating a business enterprise.

The office of the Secretary of State is usually a good place to begin when dealing with the state government, then proceed to contact the Department of Revenue and Taxation and Department of Labor.

The federal government will of course want you to report all income and activities to the Internal Revenue Service and periodically provide information to the Social Security Administration and Department of Labor.

Horticultural businesses have some special regulations and agencies to deal with. The state department of agriculture usually issues permits for nursery and greenhouse production and sales. They will probably inspect your premises at least annually. It may be a good idea to check with the local health department to see if they have any regulations with which you might need to comply. Federal and state environmental agencies have numerous guidelines which must be followed concerning pesticide use and fertilizer runoff at your business site.

Although I have mentioned the more important regulatory agencies with you which you must interact, there may be some minor ones which are specific to your locality. The

WYOMING DEPARTMENT OF AGRICULTURE
TECHNICAL SERVICES SECTION
CHEYENNE, WYOMING 82002-0100

Certificate of Inspection   No. 902

THIS IS TO CERTIFY THAT   JOHNNY APPLESEED, INC
has been inspected and is apparently free from dangerous
insects and dangerously contagious plant diseases   Inspection date   APRIL 30, 1990
THIS CERTIFICATE VOID AFTER DECEMBER 31, 19 90

Issued to   JOHNNY APPLESEED, INC
             2200 S. HICKORY
             CASPER, WY   82604

James W. Bigelow
                                           Manager

Most states periodically inspect each business engaged in production or sales of horticultural merchandise. Even in those states where strict compliance with regulations is enforced, such inspections seldom turn up significant violations if normal good housekeeping procedures are followed.

local Chamber of Commerce can appraise you on this point. Not all these agencies will affect you equally. Zoning laws have great significance when a business first begins or if it relocates, but after you are in compliance they can be put on the back burner. Agricultural regulations in some states are only a formality; but in others, such as California, they must be observed carefully to avoid citation for violation.

All these laws and regulatory agencies may give you second thoughts about going into business. You have probably heard at least one horror story reciting the dire consequences which await any business person who steps out of line. Don't be a worrier, most of these regulations touch you only infrequently and if you use a little common sense to understand the law and comply with it, your life will go on with only occasional incidents. The situation is no different than making sure you obey traffic laws to avoid unpleasant conflict with the police.

It may seem unusual to consider the Internal Revenue Service as a friend, but if it were not for the requirements of complying with IRS regulations many small businesses would totally neglect even the rudiments of financial record keeping. The necessity of monitoring financial activities would seem to be obvious to any business person but I have seen many businesses fail because the owner had no idea about the financial health of the company. The situation in business seems to be no different than with the general public, there are those who know what their financial status is and there are those who pay little attention to this aspect of their lives until a monetary calamity strikes.

Without a huge amount of luck no business can survive over the long run unless a system is set up to keep track of routine financial activities. Not only does such a system keep you appraised of the immediate economic status of the company but it can help you make decisions which will affect future operations.

Not many business people enjoy this record keeping activity. Fortunately there are accountants and bookkeepers who are happy to take it off your hands. Many small businesses owners find that it is more pleasant and more economical to have a professional accountant record and process all financial data. Even paychecks, social security payments, and taxes due are handled by accountants. A financial summary can be generated periodically to help you evaluate the financial status of your business. This is a great planning aid.

Of course accountants do not work for free. These services cost money. Only you can decide if they are worth the extra expense. I strongly suggest that if you find yourself avoiding record keeping responsibilities, seek out a qualified accountant to handle this chore. Be sure to shop around. Some accountants charge reasonable fees while others are high priced. You can talk to some in a relaxed manner while others charge for every minute you are in their office.

FORMULATE A STEP BY STEP PLAN

The object of gathering information, learning the laws and regulations, and exploring methods of monitoring your business is to develop a detailed step by step plan of action. Devising a written business plan will help immensely by allowing you to focus your energy upon individual activities at the proper time. If you attack the job of starting a business in an unorganized manner, much of your time and effort will be wasted. The task must be accomplished one step at a time in logical order.

There are so many details involved in starting and running a business that doing so can be overwhelming if it is viewed as one big task. Breaking the job into smaller portions will help you accomplish objectives in human sized bites. The process may even prove to be enjoyable as you see the problems disappearing one by one in orderly fashion.

Any business plan you formulate should have a timetable within which each specific task is given a definite starting and completion date. Of course you will not always be able to stick rigidly to the timetable. Some jobs will take more time than planned while others take less. Flexibility must be allowed in this case, and for problems that turn up unexpectedly. Your business schedule is meant as a management aid, not as a beast which makes life miserable. Don't panic each time you can't stick to the plan religiously, these things happen.

Chapter 10

SELLING AT A PROFIT

It is surprising how many horticultural growers spend less than a few hours every year planning how to market their crops. They toil countless hours trying to make their plants the best available and then neglect to implement even elementary marketing efforts to insure that the crop is sold at a good profit. To my mind, there is nothing more disheartening than seeing plants die on the shelf for lack of a buyer. A well conceived and realistic sales plan should be designed for each crop before any production takes place.

Although growing plants is the first love of any horticulturist, our concern in this book is not only with growing plants but also with selling them at a profit. The growing and selling equation cannot be said to have a side which is more important, each time you modify one side of the equation, the other side also changes. The key objective of horticultural business is to coordinate production with sales in order to achieve the maximum profits possible. This happy outcome does not happen without effort.

The old adage that all you have to do is produce a better mousetrap to have people beat a path to your door is simply not true in today's world. People expect you to make your product conveniently available to them, both in location and presentation. They also expect you to let them know how to use the product and what its advantages and disadvantages are. In short, they expect you to actively sell the product to them, not simply make it available.

There are many ingredients in a sales recipe for profitable business operation. You should forget the idea that the act of selling merchandise is comprised only of the presentation a sales person gives to the customers. The sales program of your company is affected by every action you take and every action you don't take. Your method of growing plants, location, pricing structure, and many more factors will affect each and every sale. I will now explore some topics which should be considered whenever a sales program is being constructed.

LOCATION

The success or failure of a business often hinges upon its physical location. In general, location is a more critical factor if you plan to sell at retail directly to the public. While location is important to a wholesale business for a variety of reasons, it does not often greatly affect access to the product by potential wholesale customers.

Obviously if we all had our choice of location without regard to cost or availability, there would be no problem. We would all chose the very best. This is seldom the case in the real world since we must balance the favorable attributes of a location with the negative aspects—such as price. A good location will cost more to rent or buy. Only in exceptional circumstances will you encounter the lucky situation where an excellent business location can be purchased at a bargain price.

The type of location needed for a horticultural business depends upon many factors. We have already mentioned the difference between wholesale and retail. A wholesale grower may require access to irrigation water, good soil, and roads adequate for heavy trucks while a retail florist would need none of these. A retail florist who plans on doing 90% phone business does not require a high traffic location while a florist who concentrates on cash and carry walk in customers needs to be where the people are.

You must carefully analyze exactly what type of business you plan to operate before choosing a location. And alternatively, if there is only one possible location, you must plan a business which has a good chance of success in that spot.

The place you begin business is often the same spot you will terminate commercial activities many years later. If you are likely to spend 20 or 30 years working in a location doesn't it make sense to choose this environment carefully? Even a small difference in suitability can assume large proportions when multiplied by the number of hours you will spend at the workplace over a 20 year span. And convenience is not the only factor. Think about the amount of sales and profits you will sacrifice in the same timeframe if only 10% of total sales is lost because you selected a poor location. A well established small retail nursery or greenhouse might have gross sales in 1992 of $400000.00 per year. Ten percent of this figure for 20 years would amount to $800000.00 in lost sales. This is a high price to pay for not taking the time to choose a business location carefully.

Of course the best spots cost more money to purchase, no one is going to give you a perfect location out of the goodness of their heart. The price you pay must be balanced against the potential benefits received. Sometimes the most expensive location is not the best overall choice because it may not generate enough extra income to justify the higher price.

Once several locations are found which seem appropriate for your business, draw up a written comparison sheet which outlines the benefits and drawbacks of each. Then assign a dollar value to every factor in the list and add up the totals. It is amazing how often this process shows clearly which choice offers the best value. But sometimes it won't work so well and you will have to rely upon personal preferences to make the final selection.

Considering the massive impact a poor business location can have upon your financial well being, I believe it is wiser to choose a slightly better location than necessary rather than select one which proves to be inadequate. My advice is to postpone any long term location commitments until you have the experience to choose wisely.

WHAT ARE YOU SELLING AND TO WHOM

Almost every new business person suffers an identity crisis. It takes time and practical experience to learn exactly what you are selling and who your customers are. This statement may sound stupid to some readers. They might say "I will sell anything to anyone who wants to buy it." This is about the broadest statement which could be made; and upon reflection, the inadequacy of it will become obvious. Certainly you do not intend to sell washing machines or automobiles to preschool children at your horticultural business. You plan to sell horticulturally related merchandise to a predominantly adult clientele. Even this more narrowly defined mission will need further focus in order to provide an exact understanding of your commercial objectives.

My point to be made is this: no business can successfully handle all types of merchandise and sell to all groups of people. The type of merchandise to be sold and the clientele to whom it will be sold must be carefully defined so that the business can concentrate upon a realistically obtainable objective rather than wasting effort trying to please everyone. Even within the horticultural field or within specific specialties you will need to define exactly what it is your business does and who makes up its customer base.

An example may clear this topic up a bit. Suppose you open a retail greenhouse and find from experience that spring garden plants, potted flowers, and indoor foliage plants comprise a profitable and well integrated combination of products. These products are sold primarily to middle class people who stay home and garden a lot, either indoors or outdoors. Each day as you drive to the greenhouse for work you notice a nearby fancy flower shop with lots of ritzy customers in Cadillacs going in and out. Such activity indicates that this flower shop is doing a land office business and you then decide to set up a similar shop at your greenhouse. Is this a good decision? Probably not!

Your present gardening customers and the Cadillac crowd may not prove to be a compatible mixture. It is difficult to run a fancy flower shop amidst the dirt and fertilizer piles of a garden store. And the busy season for garden plants conflicts with the largest cut flower occasion, Mother's Day. You would have to neglect one or the other parts of your business during that period. Serving two masters is an invitation to conflict.

Determining the general type of product you wish to sell is the first major merchandising decision. The next logical step is to find out who the most profitable customers for that product might be. Will they be wholesale or retail; and if they are retail, should you concentrate sales promotions upon rich or poor, young or old?

Once the customer base has been defined you may have to return attention to the product and make alterations in the production process so that the product is tailored more closely to the exact customer audience identified.

It is not easy to find your most profitable and comfortable niche in the business world! A lot of trial and error is involved and it is next to impossible to hit the bullseye with the first try. A business is much easier to operate and more profitable once you are clearly focused upon only those objectives which contribute meaningfully to success. Many business persons behave like impatient teenagers who cannot concentrate upon a limited number of realistic goals; they want to do every thing right now.

HOW TO REACH CUSTOMERS

Once you have determined the approximate clientele of your new business it is essential to find an economical means of bringing these potential customers into contact with your product. This is a key element of business success and it is not as easy to achieve as might seem.

There are many ways of bringing product and customer together. Each method has its own particular usefulness, depending upon the circumstances which prevail. I will outline some of the methods below, along with comments about their effectiveness and other important characteristics.

Interaction of location with other factors

We have mentioned this topic several times previously and need not pursue it further except to inquire how it interacts with other means of attracting customers. Obviously your business location is a major factor in determining how many and what kind of customer will visit. Not only the physical location but also the condition, quality, and other characteristics of the premises are important.

Most businesses will benefit from a location which has high vehicle traffic only if it offers an opportunity for motorists to slow down and exit the main street. And even if customers can reach your business easily, they will not stay unless there is plenty of free off street parking.

A horticulturally oriented business is normally dealing in merchandise which the customer hopes will add some beauty, tranquility, and spiritual meaning to his or her life. Dirty, noisy, blacktop parking lots make it difficult for trees and flowers to implant their important psychological messages into the customers' minds.

If your business location is not perfect in terms of exposure or accessibility, often it can be upgraded in total drawing power by installing a landscape which is especially inviting to horticulturists. A tasteful landscape setting is often the most cost effective means of presenting horticultural products for sale. You can do the work yourself and obtain the necessary plants and materials through wholesale channels.

Other methods of attracting and influencing customers will prove largely ineffective and uneconomical if the business location is unsuitable for one reason or another.

A well manicured lawn and displays of garden merchandise outdoors make this retail greenhouse a peaceful haven even though it is easily reached from a main business thoroughfare.

The inside atmosphere of a similar retail greenhouse is no less inviting, rewarding the curious shopper with uncommon pleasures.

Customers who are drawn to your location by costly newspaper advertisements may drive away if they can't park with ease or if the store looks run down. A super location with high quality improvements may allow you to spend somewhat less on alternate methods of attracting customers.

Conventional advertising

Now we turn to the means of attracting and persuading customers which undoubtedly is most often thought of whenever the word selling is employed. In today's world selling is almost equivalent in our minds with advertising. Advertising is an immense field and is the keystone which links products and services with the consumer.

Everyone seems to hold advertising in some disregard but even the most vehement detractors make use of its services daily. Almost any action which brings the customer into association with a product or service could be termed advertising. But we will limit our discussion to those visual and auditory media which the ordinary person would consider as falling under this classification.

Television, newspapers, magazines, radio, bill boards, direct mail, point of sale aids, signs, and product enclosures are only the better known methods of advertising. Every conceivable means of communicating with and influencing customers has been utilized by businesses.

You will not discover any new bombshell means of advertising a horticultural business but you can make wise choices from among existing advertising avenues.

Perhaps no other aspect of operating a business is less understood and more wasteful of money than is advertising. Everyone does some advertising just because it seems to be the thing to do. And if a business is in trouble, the thought that often pops into mind is "we need to do more advertising."

The reason that general advertising is often such a waste of money is because it is very difficult to accurately measure its effectiveness. I cannot claim to be an advertising expert but, if I were, my number one rule would be: always attempt to structure advertising efforts so that some means of measuring effectiveness is present. This is not easy to accomplish; but various tools such as coupons and contests for prizes can be used to at least measure immediate response. Over the longer term it may be possible to correlate sales volume with advertising efforts.

In addition to measuring response as carefully as possible, you can save money by observing some time tested rules of thumb when deciding where and how to spend your advertising budget. Target an audience by using the medium which reaches your customer base most economically. Local newspapers are generally the most cost effective means of advertising in a smaller town. In larger population centers this is not the case unless you have multiple outlets in most sections of the city. Television may be a glamorous way to reach customers but it is usually too expensive for small local merchants to use effectively.

Advertising space is expensive and almost every advertiser could make their budget go further by structuring messages to produce the greatest effect in the least possible space. Do not try to impress people by running larger advertisements than absolutely necessary. Take pride in your ability to get the message across as briefly as possible.

General Motors may have the financial resources to simply advertise their name but small merchants must attract customers with the promise of specific benefits. If your product is attractively priced, be sure the price is conspicuously mentioned in advertisements. If quality and selection are your strong points, try to advertise specific examples of this fact rather than simply using the lifeless words "quality and selection."

Most small business persons are not advertising experts. They do not possess any special talent for creating extraordinarily powerful advertisements. Studying basic advertising strategies and techniques in a few good books will help you become conversant in the subject and even if you don't design your own ads, it will help you evaluate the performance of those who do the job for you.

Representatives of the local advertising media will be glad to help you design ads if you are doing business with them. But these people have hundreds of customers, they cannot be expected to come up with a work of art for each account. They also know very little about your business needs and strategies. It is up to you to make sure the advertising they design is suitable for your purposes. And remember, their job is to sell advertising. They will usually try to sell you more than you can afford or need. Don't be impressed by their sales pitch, buy only what you need.

It is difficult to say how much you should spend on all forms of advertising. Every business has such varying needs and circumstances. Once a business is functioning normally without the need to announce business openings or to contact an initial customer base, it is likely that the total advertising budget for a retail store should not exceed 4-5% of sales. If you have an extremely good location then less than this might be budgeted for advertising while a poor location might require a larger expenditure.

Special types of horticultural businesses may allocate a good deal more or less to advertising. Some wholesale growers can do a good business with no formal advertising at all while a firm specializing in mail order plants might conceivably spend over 50% of sales revenues on advertising.

The 4-5% figure I mentioned above should be interpreted to include all outlays for advertising, not just the more obvious expenses for such things as radio commercials or newspaper spots.

There are commercial advertising agencies who can manage your advertising efforts. As in any other field, there are good ad agencies and poor ones. Don't let anyone handle advertising without your personal approval of major aspects. Whatever they do should be examined to make sure it is sensible. Most likely, an established advertising agency will not be interested in your account anyway; it won't be big enough to make them a good profit.

My personal opinion is that small businesses should depend as much as possible upon avenues other than conventional advertising to attract customers. Conventional advertising is expensive and it is difficult to determine effectiveness. The seasonal nature of most horticultural businesses dictates that a great majority of advertising expenditures be made in a short time; when you have lots of merchandise available and when people have an active desire for the product. Advertising poinsettias in July is a futile exercise.

Most of the advertising you do should be directed at specific events, holidays, or special sales. This will insure that plenty of merchandise is available and that people will be interested; it also helps evaluate ad effectiveness to some extent. Running special sales or coupon ads is perhaps the only reasonably accurate way you can measure response.

At carefully selected times, it is good to run a small ad with tremendous bargains for the customer. A half price sale will bring lots of business with only a small advertising expense. And it is easy to tell if you are getting response. A 10% off sale will not draw as many customers and will likely require more ad space to attract attention. The 10% off promotion may be so weak as to make it difficult to tell whether or not it was effective in drawing additional customers. If this happens, you cannot draw any conclusions about merchandise desirability or advertising medium suitability.

Advertising will likely be one part of business that you understand the least and which is less predictable in terms of results. You may never reach any accurate conclusions about exactly how it affects business. In this type of situation, the best course is caution. Would you commit a lot of money to any other project if you had no idea of how it would work? Spend your advertising dollars first on those areas where you can be reasonably certain of effective results.

Word of mouth

Satisfied customers are the lifeblood of any business. They will spread the good word far and wide. Customer

This advertisement combines many excellent characteristics: simple and easy to understand; appeal to local pride; specific benefits to customers; promises a large selection. A small ad with big impact, it draws crowds year after year.

good will is the best and most economical type of advertising your firm can utilize.

In the horticultural field, a good business reputation is like money in the bank. Reputation is so important in horticultural products and services because the difference in quality between plants or services are often not readily apparent at the time of purchase. Customers rely upon the integrity and expertise of the seller to a large degree.

This is the central reason why independent horticultural businesses have been able to compete successfully against major national chain stores. Consumers willingly pay a higher price at independent garden stores if they believe the quality and service are better. A horticultural firm must guard its reputation for superior products and fair customer treatment with its very life.

A liberal guarantee policy which protects the purchaser's interests is the first step towards customer satisfaction. Reliability and merchant good will must be a further part of the guarantee. Customers will not regard your guarantee as being worth much if it has not been honored cheerfully in the past.

But guarantees are not effective unless they represent a sound product or service which is offered by a firm with acknowledged expertise in the field. The purpose of a guarantee is to insure that isolated chance events or lapses in quality will not be at the customer's expense. Guarantees cannot take the place of good merchandise.

Not a good deal more needs to be said concerning how a business builds a sound reputation for quality products and knowledgeable service. Expertise comes only with hard work and study. Trust will result by following the old proverb "do to others as you would have them do to you."

No matter what other methods may be employed to promote your business, word of mouth will eventually be the main avenue by which new customers are acquired. Study after study has shown that if a person does not already have a favorite place to purchase horticultural goods, their choice is dictated primarily by the recommendation of an acquaintance or family member.

Considering that word of mouth advertising costs you nothing and is by far the most effective marketing tool available, doesn't it make sense that you should cultivate it to the fullest extent possible before extending customer contact efforts into more expensive and less fruitful avenues?

Face to face contact

The owner and perhaps a few key employees provide the principal image which customers have of a firm. It is vitally important that this image be one which works to the benefit of the company. Customers like to deal with a real person when they need assistance. You can help the business immeasurably by thinking carefully about the image you and your employees should present during customer contact. If you act as knowledgeable and courteous professionals, a tremendous advantage will be gained over competitors who cannot act or fail to act in this manner.

As I have stressed previously, a successful horticultural company must have the trust of its clientele. Many of the products and services you sell will not initially appear to the customer as being different from inferior look alikes. How can a consumer tell live seed from dead seed or fresh cut flowers from ones that are three days older? People must have confidence in your description of the merchandise. Any misrepresentations will eventually result in less business.

The quality of information given out is also an important ingredient of business success. Most purchasers of horticultural products need advice from time to time. While you cannot be expected to know the solution to all problems at all times, your advice must be basically correct and practical for the customer to utilize. Your knowledge of horticulture must be communicated in a way that is easy to understand. Remember, the people you are dealing with are for the most part, unfamiliar with specialized terminology and procedures. Present yourself as an expert but not as one who talks down to listeners.

The art of personal contact and personalized selling is not a talent possessed in equal degree by everyone. You may not naturally be very good at it but you can learn how to perform the essential points in at least an acceptable manner. Business owners and managers are obligated to learn how to effectively interact with other people.

A simple sign lets customers know the name of plants and the essentials of good care. Signs save a lot of time while letting people know that your business operation has professional knowledge available.

Special promotions

No single happening or event in the sales program will likely cause a significant change in how successful your company is. Success will result from numerous marketing decisions and actions taken over a period of time. But it is possible to initiate specific marketing objectives by utilizing extraordinary methods which are not normally effective when employed on a regular basis.

Under this category I am grouping such events as grand openings, anniversaries, public holidays or events, close out sales, special learning opportunities, and almost any other happening which does not take place with any great degree of frequency. The horticultural industry is fortunate in having many special event days during each year which heighten public awareness of your products. Most of these special days are associated with the floral segment of horticulture but such events as Arbor Day, Earth Day, and local beautification projects are also helpful in promoting horticulturally based business.

And we are blessed with that one great event each year which propels the public into a frenzy (even if short lived) of fertilizing, cultivating, and planting activity. Spring!

Special promotions, by their very nature, must not be overused if they are to be effective. Since they cannot be employed frequently, any associated promotional effort should be planned carefully so as not to waste the opportunity.

Community interaction

On the political and business news scene we often hear of "the old boy network." In many cases this phenomenon is spoken of with distaste, as perhaps a practice which verges on the unethical. Yet, each one of us very likely employs similar tactics to promote our personal interests in everyday life. It is simply a part of human nature to prefer dealing with people you know (at least if your knowledge is favorable) and to help those who show an inclination to help you.

I have mentioned how important it is to have the customer's trust when you are selling horticultural products. This trust may be cultivated in many different ways but the most effective means, and by far the least expensive, is to be known personally in a favorable light by a large number of your potential customers. People may get to know you strictly through interaction at the business site or they may know you through personal or associative contact which occurs as part of daily life in the community. Needless to say, trust based upon the later type of knowledge is considered more reliable because it has no direct connection to your personal gain.

Utilizing your personal community based reputation as a business asset is no sin. If your reputation was bad no one would consider it improper to avoid doing business with you; why should the reverse not be acceptable? If you enjoy community involvement, there is no better long term means of acquiring substantial goodwill for your business than to draw upon the positive image such participation can help develop.

Every town has a group of intensely avid gardeners and horticulture enthusiasts. It is important to cultivate good relations with these people since they greatly influence the general horticultural atmosphere. Each of them is likely to be looked up to as an adviser by several less experienced gardeners. A recommendation of your business by one of these local experts is sure to result in additional sales.

Trade associations and fairs

Wholesale producers of horticultural goods should investigate the advantages which trade associations, producer and marketing associations, and trade fairs can lend to their selling efforts. These avenues of business promotion are important in particular circumstances within the horticultural industry but will not likely benefit you greatly as long as you have a very small business.

Trade shows are definitely a good means for businesses to find new types of merchandise to sell but exhibiting to sell products at these shows is quite expensive. Only those who have a large amount of appropriate product to sell will find the expense justified.

RELATIONSHIP OF PRODUCTS TO PERCEPTIONS OF VALUE

Business managers are always concerned about the proper price to charge for different merchandise. I will soon discuss some conventional pricing structures in the horticultural trade but first I would like to deal with a more or less philosophical question which underlies the entire matter of price.

Many people have a vague feeling that the prices of goods and services should bear some relationship to the actual physical utility of these items. Of course only a moment of reflection will be sufficient for you to realize that this is not the case in the real world. In fact, the reverse is often true! What physical purpose does a perfect diamond or a painting by Michaelangelo serve for the common man? Yet the price of these items is dear.

My point is this, your job as the manager of a business is not to assign values to goods and services; rather it is to determine what price represents the most monetarily profitable equilibrium between supply and demand. The market will set the price, your task is to find out what that price is.

Everyone who is in business for any length of time eventually has this fact forced upon them, whether they like it or not. I hope you will accept it sooner rather than later. Doing so will make your job easier and business more profitable. In the commercial world, there are no absolute philosophical values for merchandise. It is worth exactly what the customer will pay for it; no more, no less.

Determining how much the customer will pay, although easier than dealing with philosophical problems, is no simple task. With most established products it is accomplished by observing what price the same type of merchandise commonly sells for under similar circumstances. Adjustments must of course be made for details such as quality, additional services rendered, and the like. But basically it is a game of monkey see, monkey do.

When a product or service is sufficiently different from previously existing ones, no reasonable conclusions can be made as to what price customers will pay for it. In this case, the intelligent way of determining the most profitable price is to test different price levels on a trial basis. This assignment is rather difficult to accomplish in a small business but the effort must be made in order to have any factual knowledge about the price. Larger companies often perform extensive pricing tests which can determine the most profitable price in a very exact manner.

The small business manager must often use rather imprecise methods to determine the most profitable price. As long as the methods employed have a logical basis and are consistent with one another, they will serve better than wild guesses. Two rules of thumb which I use in pricing are: if more merchandise is being sold than should reasonably be expected, the price is too low; and if you never hear a customer complain about the price being too high, then it is too low.

PRICING AND PROFIT

Although allowing the market to determine prices is preferable to alternative methods, the interplay of market forces requires a certain amount of time to manifest itself adequately. And in some cases it may be extremely difficult to arrive at any reasonably accurate conclusions from observing the results of market forces. For both of these reasons, merchandise and service prices are often set by rather arbitrary but practically useful methods. As long as you keep in mind that these alternative methods are subject to modification whenever market forces yield a more fundamentally sound pricing structure, there is no reason not to employ them for the sake of convenience.

Merchants often set prices by using a predetermined "mark up" for merchandise. In some cases the "mark up" results from an actual analysis of revenues and expenses involved in completing the transaction. In other cases the "mark up" results from utilizing certain formulas which have attained some degree of popular acceptance within the industry. These formulas are regarded as useful because over time and in many situations they have proven to yield an adequate profit margin for business to prosper.

There is sometimes a good deal of confusion about how to express "mark ups" in mathematical terms. For example: doubling the production cost or wholesale cost to arrive at a retail price is often referred to as a 50% mark up. In my estimation it would seem more logical to call this a 100% mark up. Of course the confusion arises because one person thinks in terms of wholesale price while the retail price forms the basis of another person's calculations. I will express mark up in terms of a number used to multiply the wholesale price.

Basing prices on an analysis of actual costs and revenues involved in transactions has the benefit of assuring that the business will not lose money by selling at a particular price (at least if the selling price is set somewhat above wholesale or production costs). But it has the disadvantage of not having any basis in supply and demand market forces.

Conventional mark up formulas have exactly the opposite advantages and disadvantages. They do take some small account of market forces since most other competing businesses are using similar formulas and presumably have found that the formula contains, in part, some approximation of the most profitable market price for that type of product. There is however, no guarantee that the general formulas will yield profitable prices in specific circumstances or for specific businesses. Only an actual analysis of the transaction can provide this information.

In the horticultural industry there are some very general rules of thumb for pricing which seem to work reasonably well. These pricing formulas are used mainly by independent stores rather than by volume outlets and they generally assume that freight costs have already been added onto a base price to arrive at a wholesale cost for the product.

Hardgoods such as fertilizers, tools, and insecticides usually are sold retail for about double the wholesale costs. Big ticket items like garden tractors may have a much smaller mark up. Trees, plants, and flowers are often sold at three times the wholesale price if considerable advisory service and a guarantee are included with the sale. These perishable items command more or less price as the services provided go up or down. Of course the degree of service is not the only factor which lends variation to prices but it is one of the major items.

Newcomers to business often fail to adequately charge for the special help given with most sales. Eventually they find that all these small services add up to a significant drain upon their time and profit margin. In a few cases I have found that business owners place an exaggerated value upon their expertise and overcharge for services. Neither extreme is good for business. You must analyze the situation carefully and try to arrive at a realistic appraisal of proper charges.

It may seem to some readers that a few percent one way or the other in pricing policy should not have a major impact upon business success. Nothing could be further from the truth. A small percentage change in prices often multiplies the profit percentage many times. Table 11 shows the relationship between selling price and profit for potted geranium plants sold by a greenhouse.

These figures illustrate that only a small change in selling price can affect profits tremendously. This is why you must be extremely careful when pricing policies are formulated. Profit margins often rise greatly in response to only small increases in selling price and vice versa. I have dramatized the changes in profit by illustrating what takes place at profit levels near the break even point. This area is where price changes will show the greatest effect on profits.

Table 11

Relationship of retail geranium plant prices to profit percentages.

Wholesale price or cost of production	Retail selling price	Total retail profit margin	% change in retail price from previous price	% change in profit from previous price
$1.50	$1.55	$0.05	0	0
1.50	1.60	0.10	3.22	100
1.50	1.65	0.15	3.13	50
1.50	1.70	0.20	3.03	33.33
1.50	1.75	0.25	2.94	25
1.50	1.80	0.30	2.86	20
1.50	1.85	0.35	2.78	16.67
1.50	1.90	0.40	2.70	14.29
1.50	1.95	0.45	2.63	12.5
1.50	2.00	0.50	2.56	11.1
1.50	2.05	0.55	2.50	10
1.50	2.10	0.60	2.44	9.09
1.50	2.15	0.65	2.38	8.33
1.50	2.20	0.70	2.33	7.69
1.50	2.25	0.75	2.27	7.14

The relationships between prices, profits, and volume of merchandise sold are also not well understood by some business people. It seems there is a near universal tendency among small business managers to speculate on how many more units of a particular product they could sell if they lowered prices. I suppose all of us small fish long to become big fish. Everyone wants to expand. Unfortunately some small businesses become less successful as they grow because they sacrifice profits for the sake of sales volume. Table 12 provides a look at what happens to total profits at different per unit profit margins when a specified number of units is sold.

Table 12

Total profits resulting from sales of geranium plants at different levels of volume and retail price.

Wholesale price	Retail selling price	Per plant profit margin	Number of units sold	Total profits
$1.50	$3.00	$1.50	1000	$1500.00
1.50	2.25	0.75	2000	1500.00
1.50	1.65	0.15	4000	600.00
1.50	1.55	0.05	5000	250.00

It becomes apparent from these figures that total profits can fall quickly as selling price is decreased to entice customers. Eventually we must expect that decreases in price would no longer result in increased volume because the market is saturated with product.

Table 12 is greatly simplified and relies upon volume figures which are only educated assumptions, but I believe the general picture revealed is essentially valid. It is true that the wholesale purchase price or the cost of production would likely decrease slightly as the volume of sales went up but eventually this figure would remain static or change very little. The only thing small wholesale purchase price changes would modify is the point at which increases in volume became less and less profitable.

The two examples constructed above point out the perils a business faces when selling prices are modified in response to any market stimulus, and in particular when prices are lowered to initiate an increase in sales volume. Lowering prices may be a sound decision for any number of reasons but there is a large risk that the change may cause an unexpectedly large profit decline.

Tables 11 and 12 also show that pricing variations do not have the same effect under all business conditions.

Price alterations must not be considered as isolated actions. Their effect will be felt in every aspect of your business. These interrelationships demand that each major segment of business operation be examined for possible reactions to proposed changes.

Standardized mark up formulas serve only as aids in establishing a beginning price for merchandise. With experience you will find that certain products sell well at even higher mark ups than normal while some products must be sold at lower mark ups in order to keep them moving along. There is nothing unusual about this situation, it is simply the market telling you that you must modify prices according to the customer's needs and preferences.

Some merchants refuse to handle items which, after trial, they find cannot be sold for the accustomed mark up. But I have never seen a store manager who declined to handle products that could be sold for higher than normal mark ups. The most realistic approach is to accept higher and lower mark ups as a part of life. As long as a lower mark up item is not actually losing money it is difficult to justify not selling it if it meets other suitability criteria for your business. Handling merchandise which loses money is another story, there must be powerful and good reason to enter this territory. Even "loss leaders" offered by chain stores are seldom sold at an actual loss.

ESTABLISHMENT OF WHOLESALE PRICES

The pricing discussion we have just been over referred mainly to retail situations. Obviously, wholesale growers of horticultural crops face a somewhat different situation. Although it is possible for wholesalers to use some type of "mark up" formulas, they must first determine their costs of producing certain crops.

Basically a wholesale grower adds up all the direct costs of growing a particular plant and then assigns additional overhead expenses to the plant in order to arrive at the total production cost. A wholesale price is then calculated by adding the desired profit level onto production costs.

Several variations in method are often used to determine total production costs. The personal preference of growers often determines the exact method used but certain conventional procedures are more common in one speciality area then in another. The amount of time and labor it takes to grow a crop and the space occupied are usually the critical factors which determine production costs.

ADDITIONAL PRICING CONSIDERATIONS

Your success in horticultural business will depend to a great degree upon how well you understand and apply pricing factors. The short space I have devoted to this topic does not do justice to its importance, only some of the more basic considerations have been touched upon. If you start a business, it will be necessary to delve more deeply into this subject. Books, magazines, seminars, and personal observation are the main sources of information which you can utilize. There are many technical factors about pricing which you can become aware of through study, it is not necessary to learn everything through the school of hard knocks.

Chapter 11

THE INGREDIENTS FOR BUSINESS SUCCESS

The topics I wish to cover in this chapter are many and often can be sufficiently expressed in only a few words. I believe a short presentation in outline form will ultimately prove more useful than will a long winded exposition on each element of concern. Certain topics may suffer somewhat from this brevity but readers will possess a concise list of important concepts which they can commit to memory.

Certainly there are additional points which other people might include in this list but if you can practice each of the ones I mention as if they were second nature, I have no doubt that you will be successful in business without need of further instruction.

1. Develop an overall business strategy and stick to it until proven wrong.
2. Don't be impatient, building a highly profitable business usually requires several years.
3. Study problems carefully and then rely upon your own judgment rather than that of others.
4. Be realistic, have a factual basis for your decisions. Analyze data in numerical form whenever possible.
5. Be enthusiastic, even under trying circumstances you should be able to maintain a positive outlook if you are truly interested in what you are doing.

6. Don't procrastinate. Tackle unpleasant jobs at their proper time and get them out of the way.
7. Ask questions and learn. Don't be afraid to show your ignorance.
8. Learn to think and communicate precisely. Don't leave things up in the air.
9. Knowledge is power. Stay abreast of new developments. Read and study all about your business. It is false economy to be miserly with your educational program.
10. Plan ahead and anticipate upcoming developments rather than reacting to them after the fact.
11. Make your business compatible with a satisfying personal life.
12. Allow adequate time to think and develop management strategies for your business.
13. Long term success is built upon repeat business. Treat customers fairly to promote enduring relationships.
14. Manage risk. Always make decisions with an appreciation of the risks involved.
15. Rely upon proven products, techniques, and policies for everyday business operation. Innovations should be introduced on a trial basis first.
16. Efficient repetition of processes, actions, and policies without the need for constant supervision is key to profitable business operation. Avoid "one of a kind" situations, which are the rightful domain of the artist.
17. Structure your business so that every aspect is as predictable as possible. Intelligent decisions cannot be made without a predictable atmosphere.
18. Do not overextend yourself financially. When decisions are made in a state of financial panic, they are wrong more often than right.
19. Don't allow the actions of competitors to unduly influence your business decisions.
20. Increase your personal efficiency by managing other people effectively and by using labor saving technology where it is economically applicable.

21. Control the destiny of your business by being as self sufficient as is reasonably possible. Initial cost is not always the primary consideration. Predictability and quality control are often most easily accomplished through internal control.
22. Concentrate upon business niches which most effectively utilize your expertise, inclination, and resources.
23. Integrate the individual aspects of your business so that the whole functions as efficiently as possible. If a particular aspect does not lend itself to integration, think about eliminating it.

Chapter 12

HOW TO FINANCE A NEW BUSINESS

There are many reasons why only a small fraction of all the business ventures dreamed up by people ever get off the ground. One of the major difficulties lies in getting the money together for a start. Fortunately, many horticulturally based businesses require only a minimal grubstake. The amount of money you will need to start with depends upon the type of business, how large you wish to begin, how much expense you can avoid by substituting hard work, and the amount of usable resources you already possess.

No matter how you finance a new business, don't start out too big. Limit your risk by beginning small and then grow as you gain experience. And whether you borrow money or finance the venture yourself, plan realistically so that you have enough capital to see the project through to completion.

A good deal of early expenses can be avoided if you work a little harder and improvise by salvaging and recycling useful materials. However, carrying this form of economy too far can exhaust your energy and slow down the project more than the savings is worth.

I am not a financial expert so I do not expect that the following discussion of financial sources is complete, but I do think it touches upon the most promising avenues. Whatever financial source you expect to employ, the lender will be more favorably disposed if a well conceived business and financial plan is offered in support of your application. Most commercial or government lenders have trained staff and written materials to help you prepare such a proposal. Organizing your thoughts into a coherent plan is not only essential from the lender's point of view but it is a great aid in clarifying your own vision of the venture.

If you read the newspapers or listen to news programs, the inevitability of cost overruns will come as no surprise. Sloppy preparation of cost estimates is one reason for this phenomenon but the major culprit is the impossibility of anticipating every small expense which may be encountered in a project. Your financial projections should include a fund for unexpected expenses, especially during the first years of business when money is tight and your experience is limited. I normally anticipate a 5 - 10% cost overrun for specific projects even though I have been in business for over 20 years. This is in addition to a small miscellaneous fund which I set aside for every cost estimate.

Most people who plan to start a horticultural business probably already have a job or other sources of income. I strongly suggest that you plan your new business activities to coexist for a time with your present employment. The extra outside income will take part of the financial strain off you and may provide important health care benefits.

Of course there will be a point where it is impossible to continue burning the candle from both ends. A decision must then be made to abandon one or the other. For some people this is a very traumatic event; making a choice between the security of a good job and the dream of owning a successful business is not an easy task. Hopefully your business will be so profitable that no great sacrifice in security need be made.

Another means of minimizing the money you will need to get started is to postpone some major expenses as long as possible. This may be accomplished by renting or leasing as much as is practical or by just plain doing without until absolutely necessary. Not only does this save initial capital but it lets you gain important experience before committing for major purchases. The following avenues represent the most frequently employed means of obtaining small business capital.

RELATIVES AND FRIENDS

Aside from personal assets, this is the most common source of start up funds for small business people. It should not be! You may jeopardize close relationships by using friends and relatives as money lenders. Even when the business is a resounding success and everyone is paid back according to schedule, some strain may be introduced into the relationship. I don't have to tell you what happens if you can't retire the debt as promised.

If you must borrow from family or friends, insist that everything be formally written down just as if you were getting the money from a bank. This will help to make sure there are no misconceptions which will come back to haunt you in the future.

BANKS AND COMMERCIAL LENDERS

A person might think the local bank or savings and loan would be a prime source for small business start up funds. Don't get your hopes up! Unless you have iron clad collateral, some type of government loan guarantee, or you catch them at a weak moment; banks are not likely to take a risk on you. Bankers are very conservative and like to make their money on sure bets. Occasionally some form of lending hysteria (one of which took place in the 1980's and precipitated the great savings and loan scandal) overcomes their caution. But then the easy money usually goes to slick talkers or old school chums, rather than well intentioned people like you and me.

Banks not only desire collateral, they want you to show a demonstrated ability to repay the loan. Taking possession of your belongings is a messy business (and it may be expensive), it isn't what they really like to do. They would much rather receive their payments on schedule. So even if you have adequate collateral but cannot show a steady income source adequate to meet monthly loan payments, don't count on getting a loan.

Home improvement loans

While banks and commercial lenders are not especially receptive to start up business loans, they are extraordinary receptive to home improvement loans. It may well be that you can obtain financing for certain business related expenses through a home loan. Most banks are glad to extend credit for recreational greenhouses if the structure meets certain criteria. Improvements for nursery and perennial beds might also be eligible. Loans for small garden type equipment are available not only through the bank but most all large stores dealing in this type of merchandise have a time payment program which is easy to utilize.

Home improvement and similar type loans are relatively easy to arrange and can take a good deal of the hassle out of getting the money approved for a project. But I must make it clear that providing false information for loan purposes is generally against the law.

As long as the improvements are made according to specifications in the loan agreement, you will have no problems. But applying for home improvement money and then using it for totally unrelated purposes exposes you to legal action by the lender. The improvement must be for a bonafide purpose which the lending agency gives approval. Incidental use later in your home business will not upset them.

Guaranteed loans

Because commercial banks and lending institutions are reluctant to supply small business start up money, various government agencies often act as guarantors of these type of loans. You still borrow the money from a local source but all or part of the loan repayment is guaranteed by government agencies. The Small Business Administration is perhaps the best known of these agencies but there are several other federal programs and numerous individual state and local government counterparts.

If you are located in a basically agricultural area, the local county agent can give you a line on various agricultural loan programs offered by state and federal agencies. And in cities there are all types of programs for minorities, disadvantaged persons, and neighborhood improvement. No

First page of a guaranteed loan application from the Small Business Administration. These loans are one of the most viable sources of business capital for American entrepreneurs.

matter who you are, chances are good that some special program exists to help you get started in business. It is up to you to do the footwork and locate the specific program which suits your needs best. Seldom does anyone walk up and give you the money, you have to find out where it is and then ask for it.

FINANCIAL GRANTS

Grants are the best financial aid you can receive. As the name implies, you are not required to pay the money back. It is free if you qualify. Needless to say, there is less likelihood of finding a grant than of obtaining a loan.

Many governmental agencies have small business grants available. Mainly to cultivate opportunity for disadvantaged population groups and individuals. Some grants are awarded with the idea of stimulating new technologies or to support particular industries. At the present time, the ecological movement provides the impetus for a favorable outlook concerning grant availability for horticultural projects.

If you live in an economically depressed area, there may be a good deal of economic development aid available through state and local agencies. These entities are perhaps the best source of grants for the ordinary person who has no special afflictions or needs. Loans through these avenues are even easier to obtain and usually carry a low interest rate. Economic development grants may be used to finance any stage of a business but they are commonly awarded to help businesses plan the feasibility and marketing of products or to train and hire local workers for the new enterprise.

PARTNERS

People become associated together in business for many reasons but one of the most common factors bringing business partners together is the need for money. Partners may pool their monetary resources or one may contribute most of the money while the other contributes mainly expertise and time.

Partners in business can be a good source of financial help but they want something which an ordinary lender does not demand, a part of the business. You should think long and hard before mortgaging the future control of your enterprise. If your primary need is for money rather than some other valuable asset your possible partner can bring into the business, I would suggest that you exhaust all other means of financing before becoming involved in co-ownership.

SUPPLIER CREDIT

In my estimation supplier credit is the most useful, most economical, and easiest way to obtain financing for your business. Suppliers are eager to sell you products and they normally have a ready made line of credit just waiting for you to use. They will usually extend credit if you have a good personal credit history and comply with minimal credit application procedures. Many suppliers will rely upon their personal evaluation of you if you visit them beforehand.

Remember, every supplier has competitors to worry about. If one company won't extend credit, ask another until you find someone who is more eager to do business. Credit policies vary greatly from one supplier to another. Some will give you the fifth degree while others will allow you to charge with little more than a short personal visit.

The best way to obtain supplier credit is to prepare a credit history and obtain references from your bankers and other credible people who know you. Then arrange a personal interview with the supplier, this face to face encounter is important. It is easy to say "no" over the phone but unless there are compelling reasons, the answer will be "yes" in person.

LOANS FROM LIFE INSURANCE AND RETIREMENT

The cash value of life insurance policies is easily converted into cash. You can simply call the issuing company or look on the policy schedule to find out how much cash value your policies have and then make arrangements to borrow directly from the insurance company or to use the cash value as collateral for a bank or other commercial lender loan.

If you have a personal retirement program it is possible to borrow against it unless the rules under which the program is set up forbid such action. Most likely you will simply use the retirement program as collateral rather than as a direct source of funds.

Chapter 13

COPING WITH SUCCESS

Some persons strive to succeed for years and then find themselves at loose ends when the objective is finally achieved. One way to avoid this "post success syndrome" is to begin envisioning future goals even during the early stages of your present venture.

Start asking yourself questions about how large you want your business to become, how much time you want to devote to it once it is established, and how it will be disposed of in the future. If you consider these and other important points long before they develop into actualities, you may find that the answers become evident as you make progress toward more immediate goals.

Success in business is not easy to achieve and it is a shame to see so many good people squander the work of a lifetime simply because they failed to plan for the demands which prosperity places upon them. Good fortune doesn't last forever so I would suggest that you make sure the success you have achieved is well ensured by paying off all debts and establishing an emergency fund for the inevitable bouts of bad luck which everyone is bound to encounter. Then new personal and commercial projects can be pursued if you feel the need for further accomplishment.

Perhaps the most intractable problem successful business persons encounter is the need to delegate responsibility. The very characteristics which enable small business people to succeed in the first place often prevent them from allowing other individuals to begin shouldering some of the load. No business can continue to grow unless authority and responsibility are passed on to subordinates.

Even if you do not care to have a business which keeps on growing indefinitely, it will be necessary to delegate responsibility so that you have the time to enjoy present accomplishments. You must begin early developing the habit of letting someone else take care of routine daily activities, if you don't the increasing demands of business will become suffocating.

Developing a business organization rather than continuing to operate as a "one man show" will not only enable you to have time for personal enjoyments, it will ensure that the business you build is a marketable entity which a buyer can operate without becoming entangled in daily technical details. A profitable small business is worth a good deal of money and it can be made even more valuable by developing a management and labor team which can run the business with a minimum of direction. A business should be thought of not only as a source of immediate income but as a financial asset which may someday be sold.

I hope that in this book I have provided you with a clear outline of how to get started and be successful in a horticultural speciality business. I have no doubt that there is an "Earth friendly" enterprise which will prove both profitable and enjoyable if you wish to try your luck.

But remember; business should add to the enjoyment of life rather than greedily consuming all your energies and free time. Make sure you never lose sight of this important concept. If you love plants, making money in a horticulturally related business can fulfill monetary needs without compromising esthetic and spiritual values which should provide the basis for a good life.

Suggested Literature

The following list of printed works is not intended to represent every information source available; it only provides the reader access to some quickly obtainable details about a particular field of interest.

Those who wish to find additional printed information should consult the reference works entitled *Books in Print* (for non-serial works) and *The Standard Periodical Directory* or *Ulrich's International Perodicals Directory* (both for newspapers and magazines). These publications are at almost every public library and can be used to find all major publications in a field of interest. A description of informational sources available from Andmar Press is given near the back of the book you are now reading. Ordering information will be found there.

Books

The Greenhouse and Nursery Handbook—A Complete Guide to Growing and Selling Ornamental Container Plants. Francis X. Jozwik. 510 pages. 1992. Andmar Press. P.O. Box 217 Mills, WY 82644.

Recommended Booklist for Horticultural Entrepreneurs. Free literature. Andmar Press. P.O. Box 217 Mills, WY 82644

Perennial Plants for Profit or Pleasure—How to Grow and Sell in Your Own Backyard. Francis X. Jozwik. 65 pages. 1992. Andmar Press. P.O. Box 217 Mills, WY 82644.

Magazines, Newsletters, Newspapers

Floral

Flowers &. Teleflora. Teleflora Plaza, Suite 260, 12233 W. Olympic Blvd.; Los Angeles, CA 90064. (213) 826-5253.

Florists' Review.
Florists' Review Enterprises, Inc. Suite 105, 2231 Wanamaker
P.O Box 4368; Topeka, KS 66614. (913) 273-2734.

SAF Magazine.
Branch-Smith Publishing. 120 St.Louis Ave.; Fort Worth, TX
76104. (817) 332-8236.

Greenhouse

Flower News.
549 W. Randolph St.; Chicago, IL 60661. (312) 236-8648.

Greenhouse Grower.
Meister Publishing Co. 37733 Euclid Ave.; Willoughby, OH
44094. (216) 942-2000.

Greenhouse Manager.
Branch-Smith Publishing. 120 St. Louis Ave.; Fort Worth, TX
76104. (817) 332-8236.

Greenhouse Product News.
Scranton Gillette Communications, Inc. 380 E. Northwest
Highway; Des Plaines, IL 60016. (708) 298-6622.

Grower Talks.
Geo. J. Ball, Inc. P.O. Box 532, 1 North River Lane, Suite 206;
Geneva, IL 60134. (708) 208-9080.

PPGA News.
Professional Plant Growers Association. P.O. Box 27517;
Lansing, MI 48909. (517) 694-7700.

Herbs

The Herb Market Report.
Organization for the Advancement of Knowledge. 1305 Vista
Dr.; Grants Pass, OR 97527. (503) 476-5588.

Hydroponics

The Soilless Grower.
Hydroponic Society of America. P.O. Box 6067; Concord, CA 94524. (415) 682-4193.

The 21st Century Gardener.
Growers Press, Inc. P.O. Box 189; Princeton, B.C. Canada VOX 1WO. (1-604) 295-6263.

Landscaping

Interior Landscape Industry.
American Nurseryman Publishing Co. 111 N. Canal St.; Chicago, IL 60606. (312) 782-5505.

Landscape Contractors News.
American Association of Landscape Contractors. 405 N. Washington St., Suite 104; Falls Church, VA. (703) 241-4004.

Marketing

Floral Mass Marketing.
549 W. Randolph St.; Chicago, IL 60661. (312) 236-8648.

Garden Supply Retailer.
One Chilton Way; Radnor, PA 19089. (215) 964-4275.

Nursery Retailer.
Brantwood Publications, Inc. 3023 Eastland Blvd., Suite 103; Clearwater, FL 34621. (813) 796-3877.

Nursery

American Nurseryman.
American Nurseryman Publishing Co. 111 N. Canal St.; Chicago, IL 60606. (312) 782-5505.

Nursery Manager.
Branch-Smith Publishing. 120 St Louis Ave.; Fort Worth, TX 76104. (817)332-8236.

Nursery News.
549 W. Randolph St.; Chicago, IL 60661. (312) 236-8648.

Vegetables

American Vegetable Grower.
Meister Publishing Co. 37733 Euclid Ave.; Willoughby, OH
44094. (216)942-2000.

Depending upon the policies of individual magazines listed above, the publishers may elect to send complimentary copies upon request if you indicate an interest in subscribing. Some publishers will require payment beforehand to cover at least postage and handling costs. Most specialized magazine titles are not carried by smaller public libraries.

Almost every state has nursery, greenhouse, landscape, and floral associations which publish newsletters and magazines of varying scope and quality. Local county agents should be able to advise you of the availability of at least the most important publications.

INDEX

Advertising
  agencies 144
  budget 144
  conventional 142-145
  free 91
  space 143
  word of mouth 145-148
Assets 33, 35, 174

Bedding plants 54, 68
Books 28, 76, 126, 128, 175
Business
  characteristics of 16
  definition 23, 24
  environment 16
  grants 170
  horticultural activities 17, 32
  horticultural speciality 109-124
  integrated 106
  loans 167-170
  operations 17
  opportunities 110, 123
  organization 174
  partners 32, 170
  plans 27, 129, 133
  practices 130-133
  propositions 37
  retail 56, 105-108
  strategy 161
  wholesale 56

Cash flow 50, 77, 90
Christmas trees 17, 123
Clientele 138, 139, 148
Climate
  crop 76
  local 82, 123
  nursery 74
  variability 74

Community interaction 150, 151
Competition 21, 106, 118, 120, 162
Conferences 27
Consultants 27, 127, 128
Cost analysis greenhouse 62-69
Costs
  fixed 65, 88
  operational 48, 88
  production 66, 89, 159
  variable 65, 88
Counseling 26
Crop
  nursery 73, 74
  outdoor 72, 75
  productivity 47
  profitability 37, 47
  scheduling 37
  single 57
  specialized 57, 58
Cultural system 61
Customer base 138, 139, 143
Customer contact 148, 149
Cuttings 61, 72, 98, 103

Environment
  controlled 44, 48
  manipulation 44
  world 91
Expenses
  avoiding 165
  greenhouse 62-69
  nursery 86-93

Fertilizer 68, 91
Financial
  grants 170
  partners 171
  planning 126, 166
  projections 166

records 132
sources 165-172
statement 35, 36
Flowers
annual 95, 96
cut 60, 61
holiday 54
potted 54, 55, 56, 68
Foliage plants 55, 56, 68
Freight 62, 155

Gardening activity 20
Garden
plants 50, 51, 53, 55
season 49, 53, 54
Goals 25
Grafting 72
Grants financial 170
Greenhouse
business 17, 40
climate 69
crop plan 48
cultural advantages 45
definition 41, 43
expenses 62-69
herb business 17
marketing 41-69
methods 47, 93
ornamentals 41-69
physical environment 69
production 41-69
production advantages 45
production schedules 49
profits 62-69
structure 67
technique 47
vegetable business 17, 111-113
vegetable production 111-113
wholesale 55-57
Guarantee 84, 85, 87, 117, 119, 147

Herbs
business 17
dried 123
marketing 113-115
medicinal 115
production 113-115
Horticultural
business 17
commercial 20, 21
learning service 17
production 5, 6, 9, 10, 15
products 123
recreation programs 17
retail outlets 6, 7
sales 6, 7
specialty business 109-124
therapy 17, 121-123
Horticulture
business 17, 37, 40
crops 4, 20
definition 3
enthusiasts 151
mail order 115-117
opportunity 8
ornamental 4, 8
patterns of organization 8
Horticulturist professional 4, 5
Hydroponic systems 112

Information gathering 25, 26, 28, 127
Integration
business 163
marketing 61
of factors 15
of operation 15
vertical 15
Interaction community 150-151
Investment 20
capital 90
greenhouse 47

Inventory
  assets 33
  holding area 61
  liabilities 33
  material 33, 117
  mental 33
  monetary 33
  nursery 74
  plant 76, 117
  resources 33

Labor force 53
Landscape plants 76
Landscapers 85, 90
Landscaping
  bids 118
  business 84, 118
  home or business 75
  interior 17, 117, 120
  jobs 76, 84, 85, 86, 118
  nursery 76
  outdoor 17, 117, 120
Lawn
  plugs 17, 123
  sod 17, 123
Laws 130, 131, 133
Leisure activities 20
Liabilities 33
Loan
  agricultural 169
  bank 167, 168
  guarantee 167, 168
  home improvement 168
  life insurance 171
  retirement 171
  special programs 169
Location
  business 136-138
  characteristics 140
  interaction 140
  nursery 85
  retail 106

Magazines 129, 175-178
Mail order
  horticulture 115-117
  plants 17
Management
  administrative 126
  aids 133
  financial 126
  inefficient 47
  intensive 47
  marketing 126
  personnel 126
Market
  consumer 68
  crop 135
  expanding 68
  herb 114
  survey 76
  wholesale 90, 103
Market gardens 17
Marketing
  associations 151
  crops 6, 8, 10, 11, 12, 46, 49, 55, 56
  greenhouse 41-69
  integration of 15, 61
  nursery 71-93
  objectives 150
  perennial plants 95-104
  plan 11, 45, 53, 85
  program 73
  retail 6, 7
  strategy 85
Market prices 8, 10, 13, 55, 152
Mark ups 20, 84, 154, 158, 159
Medicinal plants 17

Nursery
  business 17, 40
  container 77, 78, 82
  expenses 86-93
  field 77, 78
  landscaping 76

location 85
machinery 93
marketing 71-93
operation 73
production 92
profits 86-93
retail outlets 78, 79, 84, 86
stock 76, 77, 96
varieties 76
wholesale specialist 78, 84

Partners 32, 126, 170, 171
Patents 59
Perennial plants
business 17, 96, 95-104
containerization 98
culture 98
dormant 101
expenses 103
life cycle 98
marketing and production 95-104
profits 103
revenues 103
varieties 104
Pest control 93
Plan
business 27, 127
crop 48
financial 126
greenhouse 48
management 34
master 34
numerical 35, 36, 129, 161
quantitative 35, 37
sales 135
Plant care
exterior 17
interior 17
services 120-121
Plants
aquarium 124
bareroot 79, 80, 101

dormant nursery 79, 87
foliage 55, 56, 68
installation service 76
specialized 57, 58
starter 59, 72
Potting soil 68, 92
Prices
formula 154, 158
herb 114
levels 75
plant 67
profitable 153
relationships 152
retail 56, 84, 87, 154
wholesale 56, 84, 114, 154, 159
Production
costs 112
greenhouse 41-69
nursery 71-93
outdoor 74
Profits
greenhouse 62-69
margins 155, 156
nursery 86-93
percentage 155, 156
perennial 103
Promotions special 150
Propagation
perennials 98
plant 59
specialist 59
trees 72
Publication professional 27, 28, 175-178

Records financial 132
Recreation 24
Regulations 130-133
Reputation 147, 151
Retail
business 17, 40, 105-108
outlet 55, 64, 90

price 64
Revenues 66, 89

Sales
  busy season 52
  late season 52
  pre season 51
  program 121, 135-159
  recipe 136
  special 136
  volume 157, 158
Seed 51, 68, 72, 91, 98
Seed production 17
Seedlings 61
Seminars 27, 28, 129
Services 7, 13, 14, 15, 84, 109, 122,
  123, 155
Shade structures 43, 73
Shrubs 84, 85, 86, 91

Soil conditions 76
Special events 150

Tags color 104
Trade
  associations 151
  fairs 151
  shows 27, 28, 151
Trees 84, 85, 86, 91

Value of product 152-153

Weed control 93
Wildflower
  plants 17
  seed 17, 123
Workers
  greenhouse 69
  nursery 69

Book Ordering Information

Andmar Press offers the following books by Dr. Jozwik about opportunities in commercial horticulture. Mail order delivery to your door is available. Each purchase is fully guaranteed. Cash refunds are honored for any reason if the original invoice is presented.

The Greenhouse and Nursery Handbook. A Complete Guide to Growing and Selling Ornamental Container Plants.

Everything you need to know about how to grow and sell ornamental plants is clearly presented in this large, illustrated volume. The culture of hundreds of bedding plants, flowering pot plants, foliage plants, trees, shrubs, and perennials is covered from A to Z. Basic environmental factors like fertilizers, moisture, temperature, insects and diseases, and soil are explained in terms everyone can understand. The Greenhouse and Nursery Handbook is an absolute must for every horticulturist whether their interests are commercial or recreational. Hardback $59.95 plus $6.00 shipping, soft cover $49.95 plus $5.00 shipping.

Perennials for Profit or Pleasure. How to Grow and Sell in Your Own Backyard.

This booklet details the exact methods necessary to set up a low cost business growing perennial plants; literally in your own backyard. Or you can use the system to provide economical perennials for parks, cemeteries, businesses, garden clubs, churches, or home gardens. Every step of production and marketing is clearly pointed out. Convenient sources for supplies is included free. $5.00 plus $1.00 shipping.

How to Make Money Growing Plants, Trees, and Flowers. A guide to Profitable Earth Friendly Ventures.

This is the volume you now have in hand. It outlines the many business opportunities available in horticulture and offers the reader important preliminary information about how to choose a field of interest and how to get started correctly. $19.95 plus $3.00 shipping.

Andmar Press Order Dept. P.O. Box 217; Mills, WY 82644

ORDER BLANK

Please send the following books to me. Full payment by check, money order, Visa or MC is included.

Quantity	Title	Price	Shipping	Total
_____	**The Greenhouse and Nursery Handbook** Hardback Deluxe Edition	$ 59.95	$ 6.00	$ _____
_____	**The Greenhouse and Nursery Handbook** Quality Laminated Softcover	$ 49.95	$ 5.00	$ _____
_____	**Perennials for Profit or Pleasure**	$ 5.00	$ 1.00	$ _____
_____	**Make Money Growing Plants, Trees & Flowers**	$ 19.95	$ 3.00	$ _____

Total Amount Due $ _____

Canadian Orders must be paid in U.S. funds; add 10% of total for increased shipping costs.

Please Print or Type Clearly

**Andmar Press
Order Dept.
P.O. Box 217
Mills, WY 82644**

Check type of payment enclosed and indicate amount

___ Check
___ Visa or MC
___ Money Order
___ Cash

Name _____

Company _____

Address _____

_____

City _____

State _____ Zip _____

Phone (_____) _____

Visa or MC
Full Number _____

Expiration Date _____

FULL MONEY BACK GUARANTEE